MW00487463

Jamaica

Jamaica

Hannie and Theo Smit

Pisces Books®
A division of Gulf Publishing Company
Houston, Texas

Publisher's Note: At the time of publication of this book, all the information was determined to be as accurate as possible. However, when you use this guide, new construction may have changed land reference points, weather may have altered reef configurations, and some businesses may no longer be functioning. Your assistance in keeping future editions up-to-date will be greatly appreciated.

Also, please pay particular attention to the diver rating system in this book. Know your limits!

Copyright © 1996 by Gulf Publishing Company, Houston, Texas. All rights reserved. This book, or parts thereof, may not be reproduced in any form without permission of the publisher.

Pisces Books®

A division of Gulf Publishing Company
P.O. Box 2608
Houston, Texas 77252-2608

Pisces Books is a registered trademark of Gulf Publishing Company.

Printed in Hong Kong

10   9   8   7   6   5   4   3   2   1

Library of Congress Cataloging-in-Publication Data

Smit, Hannie.
    Diving and snorkeling guide to Jamaica / Hannie and Theo Smit.
        p.   cm.
    Includes index.
    ISBN 1-55992-087-4
    1. Skin diving—Jamaica—Guidebooks.   2. Jamaica—Guide-
books.   I. Smit, Theo.   II. Title.
GV840.S78S595   1996
797.2'3'097292—dc20   95-574
                                                        CIP

Table of Contents

ACKNOWLEDGMENTS

This book would not have been possible without the assistance of the many dive operators in Jamaica, and several of the hotels they work with. They shared with us their opinions on the best sites to visit in their area, and some provided the means to get to the sites. Several hotels provided accommodations and more, allowing us to stay overnight, instead of having to travel back home after each diving day. Because there were so many of them, we cannot name them all, but we want to say to them: "Thank you very much!" Of course, we have to thank our dive guides. Putting up with a photographer and someone taking notes all the time, in addition to guiding a dive for other divers, and being a model, all at the same time, can sometimes be exasperating, as we know from our own experience. Thanks for all your help. Lastly, we want to thank our staff for taking care of the business while we were away, and our friends who endured us while we were working on this book, who offered opinions on the photographs, and helped with editing.

To all of you, we hope that this reflects what Jamaica diving is all about, "Out of many dive sites, one great dive destination!"

How to Use this Guide

There can be any number of reasons why you bought this guide. You may have been to Jamaica and want something to remind you of the dives you did there, and would like to know about the sites in other areas of the island you were unable to visit. Perhaps you are trying to make up your mind if this is the place to go for diving, and if so, where the best dive sites are.

Visitors come from as far away as Ocho Rios to watch the famous Negril sunset.

To understand and use this guide, it will help to know how it was produced. Jamaica is one of the largest islands in the Caribbean and it is impossible, within the scope of this guide, to list and describe all of the diving and snorkeling sites of the country. So we had to make a choice, and we divided the island into five main areas where diving or snorkeling activities are offered by commercial operators. Then we asked the dive operators of each area to give us their opinion as to which sites were representative of what their area has to offer to a visitor. Those sites that received the most votes were included in this guide. The number of dive operators in each particular area had some influence on the amount of sites we included, and by no means do we want to give the impression that any one area has only those sites that are listed here. These are just a sample of what you may expect to find.

There is still a strong bias in this guide towards scuba diving, but we are aware of the fact that many people prefer to snorkel as a way to discover and enjoy the world beneath the surface. Even scuba divers can enjoy many sites using only mask, fins, and snorkel. For all those, Chapter 9 on snorkeling in Jamaica gives some practical tips on where to go.

Do not expect to dive all the areas described in this guide during one visit. Each area is at least a one-and-a-half-hour drive away from the next one, and road conditions are not exactly as you may be used to. For the exact distance check a map of the island, taking that into account. It is much more feasible to select one particular area to start with, and depending on the length of your stay, either limit yourself to that one area, or sample the nearest one to your location as well, in anticipation of your next visit. Because after diving one area, you will want to come back to experience the others.

To increase your understanding of Jamaica, there is a chapter on the history of the island, and the development of the diving industry. To ensure that everything goes smoothly, we have included some tips, so that when you leave the island you can say with the Jamaicans: "No problem, mon!"

Classification of Dives

As will be explained later, *all dives offered by commercial operators in Jamaica are guided dives.* The dive guides should have, according to the regulations, at least a divemaster certificate of an internationally recognized training agency. Quite often their qualifications exceed that of divemaster, and many of the guides we dived with are certified instructors.

Although it limits your freedom to dive wherever you like, this regulation increases the safety and fun of diving in an unfamiliar area. Also, on an island with limited resources, the medical emergency facilities are not so readily available from every location, and the licensed dive operators have the training, equipment, and the established procedures to deal with diving related emergencies.

The dive classification was made based on the following principles:

Novice divers: Those who are recently certified, or those who have only done a limited number of dives with considerable time in between. With up to 20 dives, unless you had more training after your initial certification, you would fall into that category. You will find this classification on dives shallower than 60 ft (18 m) or on those dives beyond that depth that do not require any advanced skills.

Intermediate divers: Those who, after their certification, have been diving on a regular basis but have not engaged in further training, or those with advanced training who did not dive in the last couple of months. This classification is used when the environment of the dive site requires more experience than entry level.

Advanced divers: Those who have had training beyond the open water diver certification and have been diving regularly in the last months. You will find this requirement for most of the sites deeper than 80 ft (24 m), because those dives require a good level of buoyancy control and a thorough knowledge of the dive tables. But don't fret; if you are not totally new at diving, and there is a dive you would like to do, sometimes all it takes are a couple of dives at shallower depths to refresh your skills, and you are on your way to do the dive of your choice.

A large colony of black coral on a deep wall in Montego Bay.

1

Overview of Jamaica

Over the years, many songwriters have referred to the beauty of this green pearl in the string of Caribbean islands, and up to today it is known all over the world for its lush nature, reggae music, rum, and coffee. One of the most overlooked attractions is, however, that part of the island that lies below the surface of the ocean that surrounds it. Divers generally do not regard Jamaica as a diving destination, except for those who have explored its reefs and have found it to be the best destination of all. Because where else could you do a breathtaking wall dive in the morning, enjoy the critters on a shallow reef at noon, and have plenty of time left in the afternoon to go river rafting, horseback riding, play golf, visit a great house or whatever else might interest you?

A view of the coast line near Port Maria, halfway between Ocho Rios and Port Antonio.

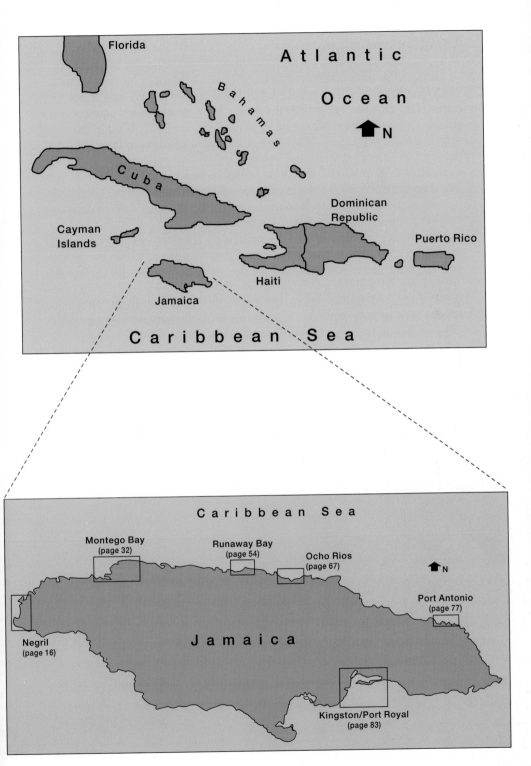

Florida

A t l a n t i c

O c e a n

N

Cuba

Cayman Islands

Dominican Republic

Puerto Rico

Haiti

Jamaica

C a r i b b e a n   S e a

C a r i b b e a n   S e a

Montego Bay
(page 32)

Runaway Bay
(page 54)

Ocho Rios
(page 67)

N

Port Antonio
(page 77)

Negril
(page 16)

J a m a i c a

Kingston/Port Royal
(page 83)

Location and Climate

Jamaica, the third largest of the Caribbean islands, is located 90 miles (145 km) south of Cuba, southeast of the Cayman Islands and about 100 miles (160 km) southeast of Haiti. It is a very mountainous country with the highest point, Blue Mountain Peak, at 7,402 feet (2,256 m) in the eastern section of the island. With a total area of 4,411 square miles (11,424 square kilometers), it measures 146 miles (235 km) at its widest, from east to west, and 58 miles (82 km) at its broadest from north to south. It is bordered on the northern side by a very narrow shelf, followed by steep drop-offs into the Cayman Trench reaching over 23,000 feet (7 km) in depth. In the south, the seabottom slopes down more gently.

The climate is pleasant year round with temperatures ranging from 80–90°F (27–32°C) in the summer to 70–80°F (21–27°C) in the winter, with slightly lower temperatures in the mountain areas. In the coastal areas, the cool trade winds bring relief when it gets too hot, and an occasional afternoon shower keeps the vegetation lush and green. Hurricane season is from June through October, but with the modern weather tracking systems there is timely advanced warning.

The water wheel at Tryall is a reminder of the colonial past and the vast sugar plantation that used to be here.

The afternoon rains keep the country lush, and sparkle on this Thunbergia flower.

Children enjoying sun, sea and sand at this public beach.

Out of Many One People

Jamaica derives its name from the Arawak word "Xaymaca," which means "land of wood and water." It is a very appropriate name for an island with over 100 rivers and many wooded hills and mountains, some still unexplored. When Christopher Columbus, during his second voyage in 1494 landed in Jamaica, he was greeted by the original inhabitants, the peaceful Arawak Indians, who lived from fishing and farming. Soon after the arrival of the Spaniards, most of the Arawaks were killed or died from exposure to diseases previously unknown to the island. Today, there are no descendants of the Arawak Indians left, but in recent years artifacts of the Arawak period have been found in inland caves giving us an insight into their way of life.

The first city built by the Spanish on the north coast in 1509, on the site of an Arawak village near the present St. Ann's Bay, was called "Seville Nueva." It was soon abandoned for another city: "St. Jago de la Vega," now called Spanish Town, which is located on the south coast. "Seville Nueva" is currently being excavated by archeologists and hopes are that even some of the ships that had been left behind can be recovered.

Spanish rule lasted until 1655, when after years of fighting, the English captured the island and made it one of its many colonies. The new resi-

A view of the city of Kingston, capital of Jamaica, with the Blue Mountains in the background; taken from Palisadoes near Pt. Royal.

Could it be that Columbus landed on this beach when he arrived at Jamaica in 1494? It probably looked much different then!

dents started vast sugar plantations that required a large work force, which was not available locally, so they brought in slaves, mainly from the west coast of Africa, to do the work. The slaves that were brought to the island by the Spaniards had fled into the hills, and formed small independent groups that never surrendered to the English. The Maroons, as they are called, still have limited self rule in their communities.

In those turbulent years of rich planters and pirates, Port Royal was the capital of the island. Located in the southeast, at the seventh largest natural harbor in the world, it was not only a base for the English navy but provided safe anchorage for merchant ships. In later years it became headquarters for the most famous pirate of all, Captain Henry Morgan, who eventually was appointed lieutenant general for the island. The city, also known as the "wickedest city in the world," only lasted until 1692 when an earthquake completely destroyed it and plunged the remains into the sea, killing one quarter of its 8,000 inhabitants. It is now one of the most important archeological sites of Jamaica and because of its location, submerged in 30 feet of water, only archeological research divers have access to it.

With the abolishment of slavery in 1838, other workers were needed for the plantations so the English soon brought in Chinese and East Indian laborers, thereby creating the foundation for a very mixed ethnic population. The national motto: "Out of many one people" reflects this very well.

Jamaica Today

Jamaica became an independent state on August 6, 1962, but remains a part of the Commonwealth of Nations. The Queen of England still is the titular head of state and she is represented by a Jamaican governor general. The head of government is the prime minister and the island has two main political parties who are represented in parliament. The capital is Kingston, still an important harbor, seat of government and commerce, and home to nearly half of the two and one half million inhabitants of the island.

The official language is English, but quite often you may hear two Jamaicans talk to each other in a language you don't understand at all. This is "Patois," a mixture of English and words of African and other unknown sources. Added to this are words originating from the Rastafarian language, resulting in, for non-Jamaicans, a totally confusing form of communication.

Today, most of the tourism industry, one of the largest producers of foreign exchange for the country, is located on the north and west coast of the island. The main tourist centers are Negril, Montego Bay, Runaway Bay, Ocho Rios, and Port Antonio towards the east. Tourism started in the early 1900s, when well-to-do visitors would arrive from Europe by banana boat and stay at luxurious and exclusive hotels and villas. Now, with the advent of modern transportation, tourism has grown by leaps and bounds and many hotels, guest houses, and villas provide a variety of accommodations, ranging from exclusive to economical, to nearly one million visitors each year, coming from all over the world.

Top Side Attractions

Jamaica is not only sun, sea, and sand. It offers a wide variety of attractions for those after-dive hours or for the non-diving relative. The possibilities are endless, sailing and windsurfing, climbing waterfalls at Dunn's River, the YS Falls or the Reach Falls, and river rafting on the Martha Brae, the Great River or the Rio Grande. How about exploring the Blue and John Crow Mountains National Park; or the caves of Green Grotto, Windsor, or NonSuch. Or go back into the past, visiting the historic great houses of the colonial period at Rose Hall, Greenwood, or Good Hope. For those interested in agriculture, there are tours offering an insight at a working plantation at Croydon in the Mountains, Barnett Estate. Then there is horseback riding, tennis, and golf. And if you still have some energy left in the evening, you can visit a live reggae concert or enjoy yourself at one of the Jamaican evenings that are offered in every resort area, giving you a sample of island cuisine, culture, music, and entertainment.

Practical Information

Currency. The Jamaican dollar is the official currency, but the U.S. dollar is also legal tender. Exchange of foreign currency is only allowed at banks, hotels, and cambios (special exchange bureaus located in the tourist areas). The exchange rate fluctuates and was at the time of printing $1 U.S. to 33 Jamaican dollars. Call a couple of banks and cambios before exchanging larger amounts; the rate varies between the different institutions. In the tourist areas, payment can be made in US currency (cash or traveler cheques), however change may be given in Jamaican dollars. Personal checks are not normally accepted.

Credit Cards. Most hotels, restaurants, duty-free stores, and tourist shops accept American Express, Visa, and Mastercard. In the rural areas bring Jamaican dollars for your purchases.

Electricity. The electricity supply in Jamaica varies between 110 and 120 V depending on location. In most tourist areas it is 110 volts, 50 cycles

A tranquil fishing beach at Cousins Cove along the road to Negril.

with American plugs. The difference in cycles should not cause any major problems with small appliances, but electrical alarm clocks will not show the correct time and blow dryers may run a little slower. If you find candles and matches in your hotel room, don't think they are meant for a romantic evening; they are a back-up in case of a brief power outage.

Transportation. Public transportation is not very well organized in Jamaica. Buses are often crowded and do not run on a fixed time schedule. There are, however, taxis, and for larger groups mini buses are operated by members of JUTA and JACAL specially for tourist travel. Tour companies also provide scheduled tours to attractions and other parts of the island.

Car rental. Most international car rental agencies have offices in Jamaica, but you will find that the rates are higher than average. Motor bikes and bicycles are also available for rent, but *beware:* road conditions are not as you may be used to and the left hand traffic might easily confuse those drivers that are new to it.

Distances. Because Jamaica is larger than people expect, distances between the resort areas are often underestimated. It takes approximately 1½ hours to travel by car from Montego Bay to Negril, a distance of 49 miles (79 km); about 2 hours to Ocho Rios (67 miles or 108 km), and if you plan to go from Montego Bay to Kingston, you should plan for a journey of at least 4 hours to cover the 117-mile (188 km) distance. Although some of the roads are called highways, most of them have 2 lanes only.

Illegal Substances. Marijuana, also called "ganja," grows in Jamaica, but it is illegal to cultivate it, to have it in your possession, and/or to use, or export it. This also applies to other prohibited substances like cocaine. In recent years, judges have started to impose harsher punishment on those visitors who break this law and quite often the penalty is not only limited to a fine, but also includes imprisonment. In any case: diving and drugs don't mix!

Tourist Information. For more information you can contact the Jamaica Tourist Board in New York at 801 Second Ave., 20th Floor, New York, NY, 10017 or phone 1-800-233-4532. On the island, in the main resort areas, they also maintain offices and visitor information kiosks, where information can be obtained.

For information about attractions and activities available on the island you can also write to the Association of Jamaica Attractions, White Sands P.O., Montego Bay, Jamaica W.I.

2

Diving in Jamaica

The history of Jamaica's diving goes back to the late '60s and early '70s, when the first dive resort was built in Montego Bay by a member of the British Sub-Aqua Club. The dive facility, called Montego Reef Divers, was operated by local BSAC instructors in their spare time, catering to visitors as well as local divers. In those days, articles about diving in Montego Bay, dubbed the underwater sponge capital of the Caribbean, appeared regularly in U.S. dive magazines.

Much has changed since then. After an initial decline in the late '70s, the diving industry has grown tremendously and today just about every large hotel has either its own dive facility or an independent operator offers his services there.

Some hotels offer the diving as part of an all-inclusive package, with one or two dives per day for certified divers, or an introduction course for non-certified divers. Generally, they do not offer full certification classes in their package.

The independent operators offer the full range of services, from daily dives for certified divers to comprehensive training up to instructor level. Several U.S.-based training agencies are represented by instructors, with

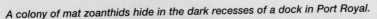

A colony of mat zoanthids hide in the dark recesses of a dock in Port Royal.

A shy hamlet, like most of the hamlets, is quite common in Jamaica. (Photograph courtesy of Terry Silsbury.)

PADI having the most affiliates, and NAUI being a close second. Most of the independent operators are members of the Jamaica Association of Dive Operations (JADO), an organization heavily involved in establishing standards for the island's scuba industry and protecting the marine environment.

This seahorse is hidden among the sediment and sponges under the dock at Port Royal.

Facts You Should Know

In Jamaica all dive operators are regulated by the Jamaica Tourist Board and require a license to operate. The requirements of this license are set out in the Code of Conduct, a document that has been drafted in close consultation with JADO members, and which is revised at regular intervals. It also conforms with the recommendations of the major certification agencies. Because some of these regulations are slightly different from those of other Caribbean islands, it is important for a visiting diver to be aware of them.

- All dives offered to visitors are guided by a licensed guide, having at least a divemaster certification, and all boats carry first aid and oxygen on board.
- No tanks or scuba equipment (excluding snorkel gear) are rented to visitors for unsupervised diving, but all operators do provide rental equipment for use on dives offered by their facility. This regulation allows tank fills for residents only, so don't bring your tank.
- You must have an internationally recognized certification card to dive. If you forgot it, and it cannot be confirmed by the certification agency, you will be required to attend an introduction class before being allowed on shallow dives.
- If you have not been diving during the last half year, an operator may request a pool or shallow water review, before allowing you on their regular dives.

Discover New Sites

Jamaica has a multitude of different dive sites: shallow and deep, reefs and walls, wrecks and caverns, but there is always something new to discover. How about snorkeling or diving around docks, pilings, or other artificial underwater structures? Or around the roots of mangroves? Although it is not commonly offered by dive operators, they may be able to inform you where the nearest interesting location might be, the possibility for access and the precautions to be taken. Photographers interested in macro photography will find so many subjects in such a small space, that you run out of film before you run out of air. Some of it is so shallow that it can be done free diving. Although not of huge dimensions, the sponges, anemones, tube worms, oysters, tunicates, and some gorgonians appear in a dazzling color array. This is also the habitat of many juvenile fish, crabs, and lobsters, and with keen eyes and a bit of luck even a sea horse might be found.

3

Diving the Negril Area

Traveling by road from Montego Bay, a very scenic drive (1½ hours) along winding roads will take you to Negril, the tourist area that has seen the most development in the last decade. Known for its white sandy beach, 7 miles long (11km), it also has a reputation for its laid back, "everything goes" atmosphere. In the early '70s it was a favorite place of the hippies, and ever since then, Negril has tried to maintain the casual ambiance. It is not always easy, with the increase in visitors and hotels and guesthouses, but still, it has a magic all of its own. Hardly any other resort area can boast a live reggae concert every night, and the beach is still the place to be and to be seen.

Roadside stand number 29 along the scenic road to Negril.

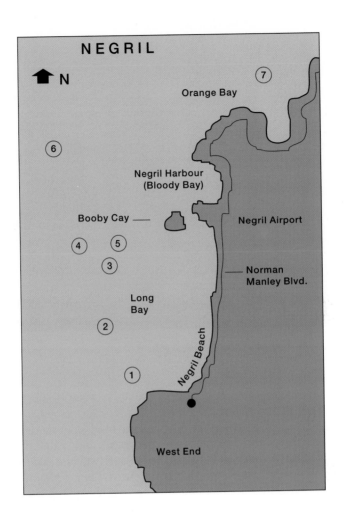

Dive Site Ratings

	Novice	Intermediate	Advanced
Negril Area			
1 The Throne Room	X	X	X
2 Sands Club Reef	X	X	X
3 The Caves		X	X
4 Kingfish Point			X
5 The Arches	X	X	X
6 Deep Plane/Bloody Bay Reef			X
7 Barracuda Reef/Orange Bay			X

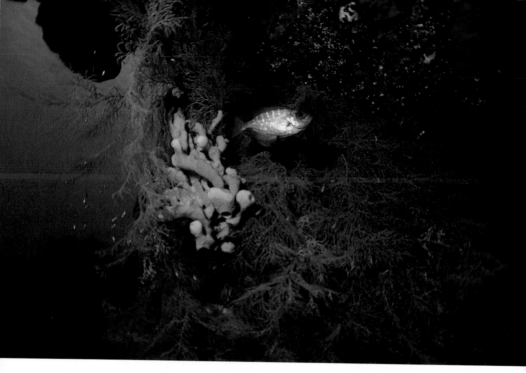

A bigeye snapper stands out against a background of lacy black coral at an overhang near the Throne Room.

And if you noticed on your way down all the road-side stands, painted in bright Rastafarian colors, offering food, beverages and crafts, be informed there are actually 157 of them between the Great River, just outside of Montego Bay, and the Orange River, shortly before you reach Negril!

In some publications its been mentioned that "Negril is for love makers, not for bubblemakers," but it is clear that whoever wrote that *did not dive,* otherwise it would have never come to his mind. Negril has some great dive and snorkel sites that can compete with any of the sites around the island. Although there are no real deep walls, like at other areas on the north coast, the reefs offer such a variety that you can fill your diving holiday with hours of underwater enjoyment. The shallow reefs are ideal for beginners and the mid-depth reefs, in front of the famous white sand beach, feature caverns and undercuts, providing photo opportunities galore. The clusters of dwarf tube sponges in a variety of colors one sees here so often, are not common elsewhere in Jamaica and the deep reefs attract fish that do not normally venture close to shore. And then you have Westend, where there is ample opportunity for shore diving.

Beyond the diving activities there is the beach, with its related attractions, sailing, windsurfing and parasailing. In addition you'll find the other activities that are offered in a resort, like tennis, horseback riding and golf, readily available.

Depth Range:	40–70 ft (12–21 m)
Currents:	None
Classification:	Novice
Access:	Boat—Mooring Buoy

At the Throne Room the bottom of the mooring line is at a depth of about 40 ft. The reef structure has a low profile, with small coral heads and sponges. On your way towards the actual site take the time to look at those coral heads a little closer. A diver with a keen eye can spot different eels and a variety of smaller reef fish hiding in the crevices. The entrance to the Throne Room, a fairly wide but low cavern, is a crack in the reef about 25 feet long and 8 feet wide. When using this entrance, you need to be really careful not to damage the coral around the opening. Upon descending into the cavern, keep your fins away from the bottom because it is covered with fine sediment, which when disturbed will immediately reduce the visibility. The walls on the inside are covered with colorful sponges and on the bottom near to the exit you can see a large orange elephant ear sponge. With a bit of imagination it looks like a throne after which the site is named. Behind this "throne" there is a large cut in the wall, where often you can find a queen angelfish. Leaving the Throne Room, you swim through a large opening forming a window of sorts, coming out into the deeper reef at 70 ft (21 m). This window provides great photo opportunities, creating a colorful frame for a silhouetted diver.

A throne fit for a king—the large elephant ear sponge after which the Throne Room is named.

During night diving, a popular activity at Westend, Negril, you may see this two-spot cardinal fish.

Continuing the dive turning right, the reef forms low overhangs covered with black coral and sponges. Photographers and fishwatchers should look under these overhangs; all kind of critters are hiding in the darker recesses. Ceros, cruising along over the sandy bottom, are a common sight, as are small groups of yellow tail snapper.

Shore Diving in Negril

Negril Westend, as the name says, is the most western part of Negril, where the seven-mile beach ends and the rocky cliffs start. In the absence of a beach, the reefs come closer to shore here, and several dive operators who operate from hotels in that area offer shore diving at sites near to their location. In compliance with the regulations, these dives are also guided dives. Along the shoreline are underwater caverns that can be explored, and other shallow and even deeper sites can be reached from the shore. This offers the advantage of immediate access to some great dive sites, while still maintaining the quality that characterizes the other Negril sites. For that reason these sites are particularly popular for night diving because the time involved in loading the boat and getting to the site can be avoided. Contact a Negril dive operator for more information on these sites.

Depth Range:	40–80 ft (12–24 m)
Currents:	None
Classification:	Novice
Access:	Boat—Mooring Buoy

A wonderful dive, mentioned by many Negril dive operators, is Sands Club Reef, named after the hotel that is nearest to it. This area consists of a shallow reef with a depth up to 40 ft (12 m), which drops off to a sand shelf at 75–80 ft (22–24 m). The reef has a medium profile and is made up of individual coral heads, soft gorgonians, and purple sea fans. French grunt, goatfish, and squirrelfish gather at the base of barrel sponges and yellow and brown tube sponges. Higher over the reef, black durgeons and blue and brown chromis can be seen.

At the edge of the reef, the schools of creole wrasse and bogas form blue clouds drifting by. Many more clusters of brown tube sponges grow on the side of the wall, which is deeply undercut in many places. Inside,

Divers can admire this cluster of brown tube sponges at Sands Club Reef.

Apart from its variety of coral species, Jamaica is also known for its sponges. These stubby tube sponges are characteristic for Negril.

these overhangs are overgrown with black coral, wire and whip coral, and a multitude of sponges. Be careful when "crawling" into these crevices; the ceiling is very low and it is easy to get caught on a piece of coral. Inexperienced divers should not enter, but instead lie down in the sand before the entrance and look in. You may discover a spotted drum, or a very shy queen angelfish against the wall, at the back of the crevice. Fairy basslets hang upside down from the ceiling and the encrusting sponges add splashes of color. Spotted eaglerays may pass behind you, so don't only focus on the reef, but also look towards the deeper water.

Going back on top of the reef, you may notice some sargassum algae. This is a brown algae that seems to be seasonal at some reefs on the west and north coast, appearing in mid-November. Come April, the winter storms have decimated their numbers and after that only individual plants can be found.

Returning to the mooring, you will pass over yellow pencil coral, a few colonies of pillar coral, and rope sponges in a variety of color. Many trumpetfish, large and small, with brown, yellow and blue coloring hang upside down among the branches of sea rods and sea plumes. At times a school of squid can be seen, lining up one beside the other, over the reef.

Depth Range:	40–70 ft (12–21 m)
Currents:	None
Classification:	Intermediate
Access:	Boat—Anchor

Although at the time of writing no mooring buoy has been established for this site, plans are to do so in the near future, thereby making it access-able to all dive operators and avoiding damage to the reef. The anchor is set in a large sandy area at about 70 feet (21 m), which is bordered on one side by a reef going up to about 40 feet (12 m). Swimming along the side of this mini-wall, we were pleasantly surprised to see a large hawksbill turtle on the bottom of a narrow sand alley. He obviously did not mind posing for the photographer and seemed to enjoy the attention. When he finally took off, we had a chance to have a look at the caves after which this site is named.

It is not often that a diver can come so close to a hawksbill turtle. This is probably an old turtle, as evidenced by the barnacles on his (her?) back.

South from the anchorage are two caverns, a small one and a slightly larger one with a narrow connecting tunnel between the two. Guarding the entrance was a congregation of six arrow crabs and two banded coral shrimps sharing a crevice with some corkscrew anemones. Photographers should be very careful: The bottom of the cave is covered with very fine silt as is the top of the cave. When you enter, even when staying clear from the bottom, your exhaust bubbles loosen this sediment, thereby reducing the visibility and your chance of getting good shots. Around the caves there is black coral, and inside, a multitude of encrusting sponges in brilliant colors and some glassy sweepers under the ceiling. As in many of Negril's sites, you can find a variety of sponges here along with soft gorgonians. On the sand flat you will see the usual occupants: furry sea cucumbers, stingrays, jacks, and some lane snappers. Divers have also reported seeing a large ocean trigger fish, big southern stingrays, and a huge king crab. At times there can be a current, but never really so strong that it will interfere with the dive plan.

The colors of sponges in very shallow water can compete with anything you might see much deeper.

Kingfish Point   4

Depth Range:	80–90 ft (24–27 m)
Currents:	None
Classification:	Advanced
Access:	Boat—Mooring Buoy

Another favorite among the local dive operators is Kingfish Point. A strictly deep dive with the mooring around 65 ft (20 m) you can decide if you want to go beyond 80 ft (24 m), because the reef is on a sand slope towards the really deep water. If you stay at the top of the individual coral heads and ridges, you will not exceed that depth.

Immediately after descending you will find a lovely low-profile patch reef, just north of the mooring, where you can spend a considerable amount of time just looking at the various sponges and the fish that reside there. Among the elephant ear sponges and yellow tube sponges, you may find Spanish hogfish, smooth and bandtail puffers, and of course the ever-present damselfish. Golden crinoids are tucked in between star and brain coral, and in the surrounding sandy area sand tilefish hover near their burrows.

Moving away towards a ridge, you pass groups of black durgeons and sargassum triggerfish, staying high above the sand. On the ridge, which in some areas has cuts in it forming sandy gullies between the coral, large boulders of great star coral are near deep-water sea fans, sea plumes, and more sponges. During the day, the polyps of the great star coral are retracted most of the time, displaying the small round skeletons. On overcast days, however, or at night, they extend for feeding, giving the colony a fuzzy appearance.

Kingfish, the Jamaican name for ceros, can be seen passing by and if there are not too many divers, they may come real close to you. These silvery fish are generally solitary and are seen on reefs and drop-offs near deep water. Grey snappers move through the gullies of the ridge, and you may see some lane snappers, which resemble grunts, but have a black spot towards the back, near the dorsal fin.

This close-up shot of a great star coral colony, clearly shows the cups, with the polyps partially extended.

The community of Negril works hard to preserve its unique environment for future generations.

Negril Coral Reef Preservation Society

In September of 1990, a small group of dive operators and concerned citizens formed the Negril Coral Reef Preservation Society. Their objective was to halt the negative environmental impacts on the marine environment and start a major awareness campaign for establishing a marine park and protected area. One of the first projects they undertook was the placement of 35 mooring buoys on the Negril reefs, sponsored by the community. A public education campaign got under way and the Society started to lobby for the establishment of a marine park and protected area. This resulted in the establishment of the Negril Environmental Protection Area (NEPA)—covering over 80 square miles and including the Negril Marine Park and the Great Morass, as well as rain and limestone forests, cliffs, caves, and blue holes—partly funded by a grant from the European Union.

The marine park zoning includes demarcation of recreational, fishing, and replenishment zones with over 150 marker and reef mooring buoys, and the program incorporates educational projects and mariculture projects as an alternative to destructive fishing and farming practices, and a unique reef restoration program using mineral accretion to establish artificial reefs. The Negril Environmental Protection Area and the Marine Park are financed by user fees, ecotourism activities, souvenir sales, donations, and environmental levies. For more information about the Negril Coral Reef Preservation Society and the NEPA, call (809) 957-4473.

Depth Range:	40–70 ft (12–21 m)
Currents:	None
Classification:	Novice
Access:	Boat—Mooring Buoy

Sometimes this dive is done as a drift dive moving from one mooring buoy to another. On one end of the Arches is a small plane, sunk intentionally as an artificial reef. Another one can be found at Bloody Bay Reef, and is called the Deep Plane. The "shallow plane" can be found just beyond the reef area in the sand at 60 ft (18m); it houses a large school of soldierfish in its hull.

On the other end is the coral formation that gave this site its name, a large coral arch, wide enough for a diver to pass through, with many deep-water fans and sponges. The reef itself features along its length many ledges and undercuts. There, nurse sharks may be seen taking a nap, and inside, black coral and encrusting sponges grow on the walls and ceilings of the caverns. Schools of creole wrasse may suddenly flee in all directions upon the approach of large bar jacks. On top of the reef are French grunts, and you may find the trumpetfish quite tame. One of them, after being photographed, approached my extended hand and allowed me to tickle him under his chin. Moray eels are also common residents in this reef.

French grunts like to hang out in groups. These are at the top of the Arches.

Depth Range:	90–100 ft (27–30 m)
Currents:	None
Classification:	Advanced
Access:	Boat—Mooring Buoy

Just beside Bloody Bay Reef, the "deep plane" is on a sandy bottom at 90 ft (27 m). A small, single-engine Cessna has been intentionally sunk here to provide an additional attraction. Actually, the reef doesn't really need this addition, because it already has a very healthy coral, sponge, and fish population.

Going down to the plane, doing the deeper part of the dive first, you will see it lying upright in the sand with the nose section covered with small, pink lumpy sponges. Because it has been stripped on the inside, you can enter and look out from the cockpit, which provides a photographer with a nice wide angle shot. When the plane was sunk, the propellor became separated from the nose section and now lies on top of a coral head beside the reef. It also is encrusted with sponges.

The reef itself has much relief, with dips and sandy valleys in between the coral heads. Along the edge are numerous bright orange elephant ear sponges, azure and lavender vase sponges, and a large variety of soft gorgonians. French grunt and blackbar soldiers are plentiful, and among the sea rods and sponges you may encounter barracudas and porcupinefish. Damsels seem to inhabit every niche there is in the hard coral.

The reef community is slowly taking possession of the dislodged propeller of the Deep Plane.

Creole wrasse can often be seen in schools at the edge of drop-offs.

Depth Range:	80–100 ft (24–30 m)
Currents:	Moderate, depending on the weather
Classification:	Advanced
Access:	Boat—Mooring Buoy

   The mooring for this site is located at 60 ft (18 m) near the edge of the deep reef, which goes down to the sandy shelf at 100 ft (30 m). Large coral heads are rising up in front of the reef to the same depth as the reef itself. The side of the reef and the coral heads are overgrown with red deep-water gorgonians and numerous tube and rope sponges.

   While descending, you may think that the visibility is not all that great, but when you get down to 50 ft (15m), it all of a sudden improves. This is caused by the currents, which mix fresh water from the nearby Orange River with the salt water to form a layer of cloudy water. This, however, does not extend all the way to the bottom, and below this layer the visibility is usually good.

The brilliant colors of orange rope sponges contrast with the red gorgonian in the background at Barracuda Reef.

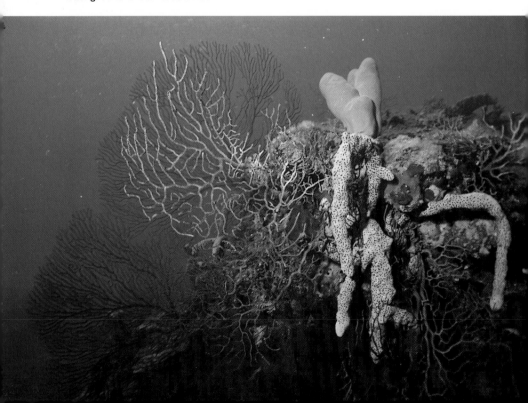

Barracudas are a common sight at Barracuda Reef, as one might expect. It is rare, however, to get so close to them, especially when you have a camera.

On the top of the reef and coral heads are healthy stands of finger coral and sea plumes. The latter, when the polyps are retracted, form beautiful purple structures in the reef, among which sargassum triggerfish, damsels, and hamlets go about their business. Towards the sand, black-looking sponges glow a dark red color in the beam of a dive light, and a longsnout butterflyfish may be seen darting into a crevice. Below you in the sand, you can find southern stingrays taking a nap. However, it does take a trained eye to spot them, because they are almost totally buried under the sand, with only their eyes and gills visible. Growing up to 5 ft (1.5 m), these elegant creatures search the sandy bottoms near reefs for mollusks on which they feed, uncovering them by fanning the sand with their "wings." During the dive, you will probably see barracudas, after which the reef is named. With their ability to hover motionless on one spot they will allow a good look, until you move towards them. Then they show how fast they can be, and will disappear like a flash of lightning in the distance.

4

Diving the Montego Bay Area

Most visitors to Jamaica arrive at the airport in Montego Bay, sometimes called the tourist capital of the island. Others may come in for a day on board a cruise ship, docking just outside of the city. Because of its central location between the major tourist areas of Negril and Ocho Rios, it is the perfect spot to stay if you are planning to explore more of the island. Not that the area itself does not have enough to offer; to the contrary, the diving and many other activities in and around Montego Bay can easily fill a holiday of any length.

Home of Jamaica's first marine park, Montego Bay is also where the first dive operations, catering to visitors, started out. Now there are several well-established dive shops, and regardless of which hotel you choose to stay in, a dive facility will either be in the hotel or nearby. The marine park, which covers the area from the airport to Great River, west of the city, has a large variety of dive sites, from shallow spur and grove reefs to vertical drop-offs, and an assortment of caverns thrown in for good measure. With the increase in tourism, hotels have also emerged on the east side of town, and with it more dive facilities. There are plans to expand the area of the marine park towards the east to include these dive sites as well, but this may take another year or so.

Top-side activities include a visit to one of the many greathouses in and near the city, rafting on the Great River at Lethe or the Martha Brae River, horseback riding, other watersport activities such as sailing, windsurfing, feeding the hummingbirds at Rockland's bird feeding station, or playing a round of golf on one of the championship courses around Montego Bay.

Montego Bay's main gathering point and center of the city is Sam Sharpe's Square.

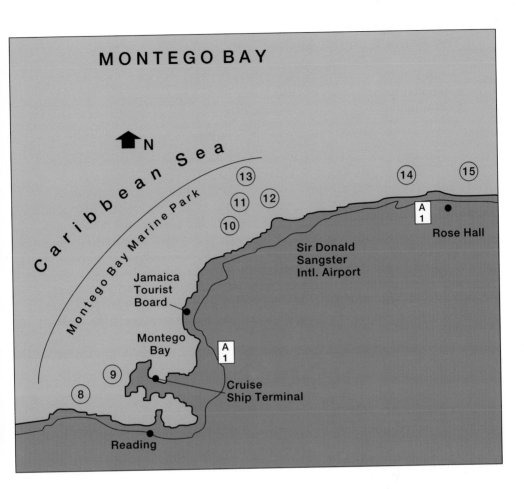

Dive Site Ratings

	Novice	Intermediate	Advanced
Montego Bay Area			
8 The Arena/Spanish Anchor*		X	X
9 Garden of Eels*	X	X	X
10 Widowmakers Cave			X
11 Basket Reef	X	X	X
12 Chatham Reef		X	X
13 The Point			X
14 Chub Reef	X	X	X
15 Rose Hall Reef*	X	X	X

*These areas offer excellent snorkeling also.

Depth Range:	50–90 ft (15–28 m)
Currents:	Rare
Classification:	Intermediate
Access:	Boat—Mooring buoy

   This site is located on the west side of the marine park. Here the shallow reef drops down to a sandy bottom at 50 ft (15m), where there is a fixed mooring. There are two ways to do this dive: as a straightforward deep dive, returning to the same mooring, or as a multilevel dive with pick-up at the next mooring. Both dives will take you through tunnels and caverns, so this site is best suited for those divers who have mastered the skills of buoyancy control and who enjoy exploring tight passages. If most of the divers are not so experienced, the dive can also be done while staying on the outside of the wall, without entering the more enclosed spaces.

   Right beside the mooring, on the north side of the reef in 40 ft (12 m) you find an old, as yet undated, very large Spanish anchor. This anchor

Divers can admire a huge Spanish anchor, its surface encrusted with sponges.

The west side of the Montego Bay Marine Park is known for its many tunnels and caverns. This one is near the Arena.

does not have much growth on it as yet, because after its discovery on the south coast, where it was buried in the sand, it was moved to this site in the park to provide more divers an opportunity to see it. In the last couple of years, small sponges have started to grow on it and patches of brain coral are starting to form on the structure.

To the east you come to a slightly deeper sand patch in 70 ft (21 m), which is shaped like an ancient arena, with coral walls on all sides. Common inhabitants of the sand area are the furry sea cucumber, upside-down jellyfish, and tobaccofish. There is another large but incomplete anchor close to the south wall. Leading to the outward wall are two tunnels that also provide access to more caverns with abundant black coral and sponges. At the outside wall large coral heads rise up from the sandy slope at a depth of over 120 ft (40m) up to about 80 ft (24 m). These massive heads are covered with large black coral colonies and tube, rope and elephant ear sponges. Sightings of eagle rays are quite common here, and in the deeper water large mutton snappers—and sometimes a nurse shark—may pass by. A group of gray snappers can be found in the shallow reef on the west side of the mooring where the safety stop can be used for a final look at the shallower coral heads and its inhabitants.

If you are doing a multilevel dive, you will continue the dive from the wall towards the next mooring. On your way, Harry, the large resident barracuda who cruises the edge of the wall and the shallow reef, may make an appearance, but be sure to look up towards the surface once in awhile, otherwise you'll miss him. You pass by the Window and Duppy's Hole, an area with more tunnels and caverns, that forms a separate dive site. In some of the tunnels you will find the rare orange "sclero sponge," one of the few hard, reef building sponges, which are normally only observed at much greater depth. The last 10 to 20 minutes, depending on your air consumption, are spent in the shallow reef leading to the mooring at the Classroom, so called because it is ideal for training dives. The safety stop is spent swimming around the shallow coral with a large colony of pillar coral near the mooring as a prominent landmark. Among the permanent tenants of that area, you will find a balloonfish hiding among the soft gorgonians in the company of a butter hamlet, and a fringed filefish blending in with the sea rod near the mooring.

Look who is looking! A queen conch comes out to see who dared to disrupt its peace. ▶

Garden of Eels

Depth Range:	20–80 ft (7–24 m)
Currents:	None
Classification:	Novice
Access:	Boat—mooring buoy

At this site, a big sand avenue slopes from 20 ft (7 m) to deep water. At the shallow end, the surrounding coral forms mini walls that go up to the surface. Towards the deep end, the coral reef has less profile and again forms a little wall starting at 50 ft (15 m), going down to 90 ft (28 m).

Two different dives are possible at this site. The deeper one crosses the coral reef going towards the wall, where sponges, black coral, and a variety of plate coral draw your attention. Over the top of the wall you'll see schools of creole wrasse and bar jacks and below, over the sandy bottom, frequently a mutton snapper can be seen, slowly swimming by. Ceros are present on every dive. The coral head that lies just off the wall has schools of grunt and you may want to look for the big green moray that lives in

the area. Generally, the maximum depth will be kept at 80 ft (24m) and as a multilevel dive, you return to the shallows along the edge of the sand avenue. Here you can observe the large colonies of garden eels after which this site is named. A garden eel is a small type of couger eel that lives in holes in the sand. But be careful not to get too close, otherwise they will retreat in their holes and if you stir up the sand with your fins, you may actually bury them and they'll spend the rest of the day making a new passage to the surface. Conchs, sea cucumbers, electric rays, flounders and jacks can also be seen in this area.

The shallow dive concentrates on the marine life found up to 40 ft (12m). It is suited to the novice as well as for the experienced divers; photographers will run out of film and snorkelers can explore the shallow reef, which is teeming with a large variety of fish, invertebrates, and coral. From the mooring you take a left turn, over the medium profile reef in which lettuce sea slugs are feeding on algae, and where the tentacles of golden and beaded crinoids protrude from the coral heads. Azure vase sponges are next to green rope sponge and yellow tube sponges are beside

A juvenile bridled burrfish, with iridescent eyes, likes the sandy areas of the Garden of Eels.

Can you identify this one?

a coral head that seems to be covered on the underside with orange icing sponge. On the sandy areas you may find the tracks of the red heart urchin or see a tiger tail sea cucumber coming out from under a coral head, sweeping the sand like a vacuum cleaner hose, to find food. Then you turn right towards the sand, where the hundreds of garden eels, resembling turtle grass, move back and forth. Farther are queen conch, milk conch, and the West Indian fighting conch. Sometimes a cushion sea star can be found and, depending on the time of the year, a couple of rare magnificent urchins, with their striped spines, wander around between rosy razorfish.

South of the mooring there are shallow coral walls with a vast number of the regular tropicals near the top. Halfway down are large trumpetfish and different types of grunts, and you may see a queen or French angelfish in one of the crevices. On the bottom are the burrows of the mantis shrimp, which share them with colon and bridled gobies. At the end of the dive, see if you can identify the tiny (less than 1 inch or 2.5 cm) fish with a gold pattern, that hangs around the top of the mooring. We couldn't!!

Depth Range:	40–80 ft (12–24 m)
Currents:	Light to moderate at times
Classification:	Advanced
Access:	Boat—mooring buoy

James Jones mentioned an underwater cave in his novel *Go to the Widowmaker,* but this one, named after it, luckily does not live up to the reputation and has not, as far as it is known, produced any widows! But nevertheless it gives an extra thrill to this fascinating dive. The mooring for this site is on a large sand area in 50 ft (15 m), which slopes towards the deeper reef between two sections of the wall in Montego Bay. When going down the slope, take a left turn, and make sure you watch your depth

A diver prepares to enter Widowmakers Cave.

These glassy sweepers at the top of Widowmakers Cave are right over the ascending bubbles of the divers leaving the cave. They must like bubble baths!

gauge, as the bottom of the wall varies in depth and it is very easy to end up too deep. The side of the wall is covered with big colonies of black coral, orange rope sponges, and the red deep-water sea fans.

On all deeper dives, especially on a wall, it is a good idea to bring a dive light along, so you can appreciate the variety of color among the different sponges and corals, which otherwise may appear to be dull brown or black. After a couple of minutes you come to a vertical, narrow crack in the wall, which forms the entrance to Widowmakers Cave. In front, a small coral head separates the area from the deeper drop-off and a large school of silvery blue bogas can be observed swimming around it. Schoolmaster snappers may be seen at the top of the entrance.

Inside the tunnel leading to the cave, there is wire coral with, in the beam of your dive light, red polyps, and the walls are covered with multicolored sponges, including the big orange sclero sponge also found inside the Canyons. The cave itself is not very large, but while going up through the chimney-like passage to the shallow reef, look inside some of the other small cracks that radiate out from the cave. Schools of glassy sweepers hide in these dark recesses and their bodies create golden accents as you shine your light on them. Keep your hoses and gauges close to you, so you do not get caught in or damage the coral. Exit onto the reef at about 40 feet (12 m), where, on your way back to the boat, you can observe stands of pencil coral, porcupine- and balloonfish, trumpetfish, hamlets, wrasses, parrotfish, black ball sponges, and sea fans.

Montego Bay Marine Park

Although an area in front of the Montego Bay main hotel strip had been declared a Protected Area in 1974, the protection existed only on paper, the boundaries were never marked, and the regulations were never enforced. In the early 1980s, local divers and dive operators were getting very concerned about the level of reef degradation they saw every day, and they started their own protection program. They also encouraged the government to do something on an official level. In mid-1980 the minister of tourism formed a Marine Park Action Committee, which resulted in a project proposal to establish a marine park. A plan was formulated to develop a system of national parks and protected areas (the PARC Project) and the Montego Bay Marine Park was the first pilot park.

It covers the area from the airport in the north to the Great River in the west of Montego Bay. The park was officially opened in July 1992 and since then mooring buoys and boundary markers have been installed, rangers patrol the area, and spearfishing has been banned from the park. At the same time a training program was developed, to assist the displaced fishermen in learning new skills and finding employment in a different occupation. A zoning plan has been established to address the impact that the different user groups have on the park. Also, an extensive public education program got underway with a goal to make the Montego Bay citizens more aware of the importance of the marine environment and the protection thereof. The effect of destructive environmental practices on land, which influences to a large extent the state of the reefs, has been emphasized.

For more information about the park and how you can assist write to: Montego Bay Marine Park, P.O. Box 67, Montego Bay, Jamaica, W.I.

Depth Range: 50–80 ft (15–24 m)
Currents: Moderate depending on the weather
Classification: Novice
Access: Boat—Mooring buoy

Located east of Widowmakers Cave, this dive site provides an opportunity to stay either on the top of the wall at 50 ft (15 m), or to travel along it at a depth up to 80 ft (24 m), depending on the experience of the divers.

Giant basket sponges like this one are a dominant feature of Basket Reef. ▶

◀ *The rangers of the Montego Bay Marine Park on one of their regular patrols of the area.*

At both levels there is a lot of interesting marine life and action. Schools of fish tend to congregate near the edge of the reef to feast on the plankton and other nutrients brought in with the current. The blues and purple of the bogas, chromis, and creole wrasse mingle with the silver and yellow of the bar jacks and yellowtail snappers to delight you, and if you move slowly and take your time they will let you come quite close. Basket or barrel sponges of all sizes, which give this site its name, are scattered over the reef, where parrotfish, rock beauties, squirrelfish, and blackbar soldierfish compete for space with the many damsels. One sponge in particular has grown to a height of at least 5 feet (1.5 m) and a diameter at least that or more. Yellow tube sponges, purple sea fans, and the large colonies of pale yellow pencil coral create a colorful background. Over all this hover the black durgeons, and small schools of blue tangs mixed with doctorfish cruise the reef.

Going over the edge, orange rope sponges, black coral trees, and red deep-water sea fans adorn the wall. The plate coral creates niches and crevices in which lobster and spider crabs hide, and once again, with your light you'll see the many different sponges that cover the inside and some of the other critters that share the hideout. Dolphins have been seen passing by, and on occasion, they use the big barrel sponges to scratch their backs.

Depending on the strength of the current, you will return to the same mooring buoy, or be picked up at the next one located near The Point. During your safety stop, keep your eyes open. Small schools of bar jack like to hang around the mooring line, which also forms the base for a small marine community by itself: tiny snails and clams are side by side with hydroids, tunicates, little sponges and algae. Juvenile trumpetfish try to blend in, and you may see other small fish that are difficult to identify, because in their adult form they probably look totally different! Don't hold on to the mooring line with your hands, because some of these small, beautiful creatures, like the hydroids, have a mighty sting in them!

Blackbar soldierfish and squirrelfish hide between sponges under a ledge at Basket Reef. ▶

Depth Range:	35–40 ft (10–12 m)
Currents:	Moderate depending on the weather
Classification:	Intermediate
Access:	Boat—Mooring buoy

This beautiful, low-profile, shallow reef is located opposite the former Chatham Hotel. When descending onto the sand area at the mooring site, the surrounding reef area looks like an undulating, tan-colored carpet. Upon closer examination, the vibrant colors of the creatures that inhabit it create a beautiful pattern in one of nature's many underwater creations. Imagine an artist with an assortment of different colors, throwing them at random onto a beige-colored canvas. This is the impression you get when you come close to Chatham Reef.

Many soft gorgonians, such as sea rods, sea plumes, and sea whips, cover the area to make up the background. Colorful sea fans, sponges, and fish provide the splashes of color, and between them is the white sand that hides so many creatures. Lie down for awhile, and watch the theater that unfolds. In front of you there are the tracks of the heart urchin, a sea urchin that lives beneath the sand and only comes up at night. Nestled

Huge stands of soft gorgonians are abundant at Chatham Reef.

The many different species of gorgonians represented at Chatham Reef are clearly visible in this photograph.

between the spines on the underside of the urchin, you will find its tenant, a white albino crab. Well, you have to look carefully; it is smaller than your little fingernail! Then, what moves there ahead of you? It is a peacock flounder, trying to look inconspicuous and a hermit crab is busy digging in the sand. In the distance you can see a sandtilefish performing his dance for you. Not moving too far away from his hideout, consisting of a mound of coral rubble, he is ready to slip away if you get too close.

Shallow dives are great for watching the action in the reef, because you can take the time to observe up close all that is happening. If you can tear yourself away from the sand theater, move on to the reef. Count how many different sponges you can find and try to identify the variety of soft gorgonians. Most gorgonians have their polyps extended, so you can easily observe their structure. With your remaining time—and remember, most dive operators require you to leave at least 500 psi of pressure in your tank—watch the fish. Small schools of French grunt drift between the coral and rock beauties dart in and out of the coral heads. Sometimes a small graysby or coney will use a sponge as a resting place, disappearing upon your approach. Doctorfish move about, but the photographer can always find a damsel or hamlet willing to pose. While ascending you may see a moon jelly; even these are worthy of closer attention as inside the transparent bell tiny fish find refuge.

Depth Range:	80–110 ft (24–33 m)
Currents:	Moderate to strong
Classification:	Advanced
Access:	Boat—mooring buoy

Near very deep water, this dive site has the benefit of the ocean currents, bringing clear water and nutrients into the reef. The visibility therefore is nearly always excellent and the plankton in the water attracts many fish, creating the ultimate wall dive.

The mooring is on a sandy area at 50 ft (15 m) from where the reef slopes down to the wall, which starts at 70 ft (18 m). Turning against the current that comes from Basket Reef, contrary to the direction of the northeasterly

A diver glides over a dense growth of sponges and red sea fans at the Point.

48

Gorgonians have their polyps extended to feed on the steady current at the tip of The Point.

trade winds, the reef forms a point going out into deep water. Following the edge of the reef, groups of sargassum triggerfish can be seen among the other schooling fish that are so plentiful at this site. Brown trumpet sponges are clustered together, giving the appearance of organ pipes. Continuing the dive, you end up at the tip of The Point, at 90 ft (28 m), and going around it, you'll see the wall below you plunging down beyond the edge of visibility to at least 300 ft (90 m). Swimming in seemingly bottomless blue water always gives an eerie feeling to even the most experienced diver.

The reef and sides of the wall have deep-water gorgonians, some black coral and many orange elephant ear sponges. On the deep side there are schools of yellowtail snappers, and quite often horse-eye jacks, bar jacks, barracudas, and solitary ceros pass by several times on every dive. In the reef area green moray eels, black durgeons, and parrotfish can be found. This is a "must" dive for all experienced divers.

49

Chub Reef 14

Depth Range: 40–60 ft (12–18 m)
Currents: Rare
Classification: Novice
Access: Boat—anchor

What do you expect to see at a site named Chub Reef? Chubs of course! Well, there are plenty here, big ones and small ones, gray ones and silvery ones, all waiting for a handout. For the last few years dive operators have been feeding the Bermuda chubs in this area and now, these normally shy fish will come very close, expecting a snack. The sloping sandy area at the end of a shallow spur and groove reef is interspersed with large coral heads, and provides a safe anchorage for the dive boat, avoiding damage to the fragile coral. Once the boat has anchored in the sand, the chubs, alerted by the sound of the engines, will come

Chubs circle a diver at Chub Reef, waiting for a handout.

A spotted drum nearly disappears among all the colorful sponges.

towards the spot to await the arrival of the divers. While the divers descend toward the bottom at 40 ft (12 m), the chubs circle them in vast numbers and will follow during the whole dive.

The coral heads, made up of plate coral, star coral, and sheet coral, are the habitat for the yellow and purple fairy basslets, squirrelfish, glasseye snappers and French grunts. If you look closer, you may discover an octopus, which is primarily a nocturnal animal but sometimes can be seen during the day. He is a master of disguise, so it takes a keen eye to spot him. All around, the sandflat is covered with manatee grass and other assorted algae. You are sure to find the more common occupants of this community: yellow stingrays, the always dirty-looking donkey dung sea cucumber, the furry sea cucumber, and a variety of mollusks that find their food in the sand. In the far distance, a large school of juvenile horse-eye jacks mingles with yellowfin mojarras and several large mutton snappers can be seen, seemingly undisturbed by the divers, but always at a safe distance. The small gathering of gray snappers, apparently residing near one of the coral heads, displayed the same prudent behavior.

And, if by chance you brought your camera with a macro outfit to this dive, instead of a wide angle lens or 35 mm, there are tiny coral heads in the sand with anemones, cleaning Pederson shrimp and arrow crabs, so you still can take back some great images.

Depth Range:	20–45 ft (7–14 m)
Currents:	Rare
Classification:	Novice
Access:	Boat—anchor

Named after the famous great house that overlooks the sea just a couple of miles east of Montego Bay, this shallow reef is teeming with marine life. This is a dive you should not miss.

At the beginning of the dive, you'll come over a low-profile reef at 40 ft (12m) from where a large pillar coral rises to the surface. Because of its size, it has been named "Fairy Castle" by the local dive operators.

◀ *This massive colony of pillar coral is aptly named "Fairy Castle" and you can find it at Rose Hall Reef.*

This "Fairy Bridge" connects two reef sections at Rose Hall Reef. ▶

Around it you will encounter some soft gorgonians; the coral heads consist of brain, star, finger coral, and small colonies of cactus coral. Schools of blue chromis hover over the reef and small groups of mahogany snappers can be seen in the distance. Closer up you may see the red-spotted hawkfish and, hiding in between the corals, a scorpionfish.

Moving toward shallower water, the reef is divided by sand channels, with the coral walls descending from the top of the reef, sometimes at less than 10 ft (3 m) below the surface, to the sandy bottom at 30 ft (9 m). This creates an intricate system of tunnels where you can swim over, go through, or just look in to discover all the creatures that call it home. On the top, elkhorn coral can be seen with, at its base, squirrelfish and blackbar soldiers. Groups of goatfish are feeding, and some porcupinefish float under the "antlers" of the coral. A large mutton snapper may cruise by with his little pals, two silvery bar jacks. On the coral wall, it takes a sharp eye to spot the minute spinyhead blenny, but the large stingray that sometimes sleeps in one of the sand channels is hard to overlook, because it measures at least 5 ft (1.5 m) across. Still in very shallow water you come across the "Fairy Bridge," a coral bridge that connects two sections of reef over a sandy "river."

This type of reef is a natural habitat for nurse sharks, so you can expect to see one here, dozing under the overhangs that have been created by the plate and sheet coral of the mini walls. Darting in and out of the crevices are French and blue-striped grunts, and sailors' choice, an uncommon type of grunt that is very shy and will retreat upon your approach. A look inside the small caverns will reveal glasseye snappers and glassy sweepers, sharing their home with spotted spiny lobsters. Trumpetfish try to blend in with the brown corky seafingers, waiting for an unsuspecting victim that may pass by. Don't worry, divers are a little too big for them! On your way back to the boat, you may encounter a spotted moray or two, see coneys in different color phases, and many other small and larger animals that find shelter and food in this healthy reef.

5

Diving the Runaway Bay Area

Traveling east from Montego Bay on the north coast toward Runaway Bay, you pass by a couple of historic places. One of the first towns you enter is Falmouth, a major port in the colonial days, which still has many buildings dating back to that era. There is an on-going effort to preserve them for generations to come. One of the next stops you should make is where Columbus first landed in Jamaica in 1492. An open air exhibition and plaque marks the spot near Discovery Bay. Continuing on to Run-

A diver cruises the reef behind a massive colony of pillar coral at the classroom in Montego Bay.

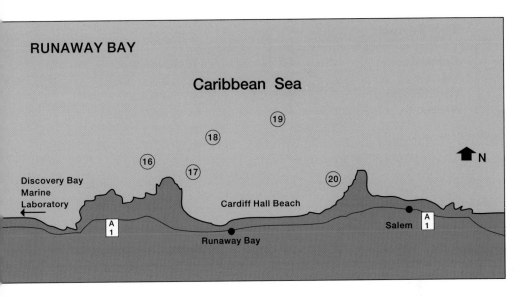

RUNAWAY BAY

Caribbean Sea

Discovery Bay Marine Laboratory

Cardiff Hall Beach

Salem

Runaway Bay

N

Dive Site Ratings	Novice	Intermediate	Advanced
Runaway Bay Area			
16 The Canyon	X	X	X
17 *Reggae Queen*	X	X	X
18 Pocket's Reef			X
19 Ricky's Reef			X
20 Silver Spray*	X	X	X

*This area offers excellent snorkeling also.

away Bay, you'll pass a bauxite plant (one of the other important earners of foreign exchange for the country). And beyond the major concentration of dive operators in Runaway Bay, after the village of Priory, you will come to New Seville, the site of major excavations of Arawak, Spanish, and English settlements.

As to the diving in this area, do not expect to pick up any golden doubloons or jewelry, dropped overboard from Spanish galleons. If there ever were any, they are now buried deep under coral and sediment. Nevertheless, the diving here is outstanding, with wrecks (new ones!), breathtaking walls, and very pretty shallow reefs.

Depth Range:	40–50 ft (12–15 m).
Currents:	None to moderate
Classification:	Novice
Access:	Boat—mooring buoy

The Canyon consists of a very deep cut in the reef, forming two vertical walls starting at 35 feet (10 m), going down as deep as 140 ft (42 m), and only 20 feet (7 m) apart at its narrowest. The sides of this impressive formation consist of plate, sheet, cactus coral and spiraling down, wire coral. In between are small brown elephant ear sponges and some deep-water fans. A school of gray snappers resides in the crevices at 55 ft (16 m) and you may see Spanish grunts and spotted eaglerays "flying" along the wall.

A divemaster leads a group of divers over the top of the Canyon. Note the beautiful stand of pencil coral in the foreground.

A cluster of brown tube sponges and some pencil coral on the wall of the Canyon.

Creole wrasse mix with bogas around the top of the second wall and a large school of enormous chubs will pass by on several occasions during the dive. They keep their distance from the divers, and their shyness is probably the reason that they could grow to the size they are! The top is covered with large colonies of pencil and finger coral, providing hiding places for moray eels, and the smaller damsels, wrasses, and hamlets swim among brown leathery barrel sponges. On several spots you may observe a cleaning station in operation, where juvenile wrasse or Spanish hogfish pick the parasites from a creole wrasse, while the next customer patiently waits his turn.

Moving back to the mooring you'll pass over some large sandy areas where garden eels, resembling turtle grass, move with the water motion. The uncommon magnificent sea urchin also frequents this area.

57

Depth Range:	50–60 ft (15–18 m).
Currents:	Rare
Classification:	Novice
Access:	Boat—mooring buoy

The *Reggae Queen,* a 100-ft tugboat with a wooden hull, has had a checkered past. After her career as a tugboat ended, she was converted to a floating disco that was scheduled to leave the port of Montego Bay a few evenings each week to provide a different type of entertainment for the visitors. The maiden voyage, after the conversion, was besieged by technical problems and there was a two-hour delay before she finally left the harbor. Very soon thereafter, the owners realized that the *Reggae Queen's* days were over and she was left to rot in shallow water. In early 1993, she was towed to Runaway Bay, where she was sunk to create an artificial reef. Subsequent storms broke up the wreck and the top section lies scattered over the reef.

It was a strange experience, having danced to reggae music on her deck on the maiden voyage, to now see it under water, with the only dancing going on being a flounder shuffling over the planks to the sound of our air bubbles rising to the surface.

An eerie view of the last resting place of the Reggae Queen.

A diver is just about ready to explore the inside of the Reggae Queen.

The wreck lies upright in the sand in between two reef areas. The down-current side shows very little growth, but the up-current side is already covered with small sponges and giant tunicates. Hovering over the wreck is a large school of blue chromis, bogas, and creole wrasse, and on the deck black feather coral has started to grow. Corkscrew anemones provide a home to Pederson shrimp, which in turn provide cleaning services for fish passing by, like the blackbar soldierfish and different species of par-rotfish that swim over and through the remains of the tugboat. At the stern of the wreck moving to the northeast you can see two perfectly round black ball sponges and yellow goatfish stirring up the sand. Southern stingrays have also been reported cruising the adjacent areas.

In the reef you can see clusters of yellow tube sponges and green rope sponges covered with tiny zoanthids. In the distance a large, resident por-cupinefish may appear, and graysbys sun themselves beside the colonies of pencil coral. If you take a good look around, you may see banded coral shrimp, and you should also watch for a large colony of sea rods. Some of these are covered with large numbers of sponge brittle stars.

Depth Range:	90–120 ft (27–36 m)
Currents:	Light
Classification:	Advanced
Access:	Boat—mooring buoy

Just to the northwest of the *Reggae Queen,* the reef ends with a wall at 80 ft (24 m) dropping down to over 200 ft. This is a magnificent dive, named after the divemaster who discovered it more than a decade ago. Clifton Hamilton, nicknamed Mr. Pocket or Mr. P. for short, is one of the oldest divemasters in the area, and is happy to share his years of experience with divers when taking them out to "his" reef.

While descending at the mooring, focus on a spot in the reef just north of the mooring line attachment. There is a cluster of bright azure vase sponges, to the left an orange elephant ear sponge, and behind it a large red sea fan. Moving from there to the wall, you'll find it totally covered with more elephant ear sponges, huge deep-water sea fans, clusters of brown and yellow

Brilliant orange elephant ear sponges and yellow tube sponges adorn the wall at Pocket's Reef.

Divers enjoy the thrill of the deep water at the drop-off at Pocket's Reef.

tube sponges and stands of black coral in between. Actually, more than 7 types of black coral can be identified at this site. In Jamaica, black coral is protected by law, which means that it is illegal to take it, sell it, or have in your possession. It takes a colony more than 75 years to form a base with a diameter of ⅓ of an inch (0.8 cm), so you can imagine how old some of these colonies are to have grown to the size you can see here.

Large schools of fish go back and forth, and ceros and bar jacks pass overhead. Rainbow jacks are seen regularly and sometimes you may encounter an ocean triggerfish. According to Mr. Pocket, there used to be a large school of them at this site in the early eighties, but over the years most of them have disappeared. After cruising along the wall for a while at 90 ft (27 m) the dive continues on the shallower reef plateau at 50 ft (15m). Here grunts mingle with goatfish and blackbar soldierfish, among the large variety of sponges and hard coral. Damsels will fiercely defend their territory and will try to attack when you come too close. On your way back to the mooring you may come across some of the top sections of the *Reggae Queen,* which lie scattered over the sandy area.

Discovery Bay Marine Laboratory

Jamaica's coral reefs are among the best studied in the world, thanks to Tom Goreau, Sr., a professor of marine science at the University of the West Indies and professor of biology for the State University of New York. Professor Goreau spent many years diving and doing research on the corals in the reefs around Jamaica, and he was instrumental in attracting funding for the establishment of a marine laboratory on the north coast in Discovery Bay. Although he died shortly after the opening, his wife Nora and son Tom Goreau, Jr. continued his work and now the marine laboratory is host to scientists from around the globe, coming to study the various corals and sponges. One of the exciting events was the discovery of sclero-sponges, a hard-reef-building sponge, the only sponge that deposits silica and calcium carbonite. It was found not only in deep water but also in caverns and deeply shaded areas. Divers can observe this sponge in several of the buttress caverns found on the north coast. Besides providing research opportunities, the marine laboratory also houses and provides support for the only recompression chamber in the island. This chamber serves not only the divers at the institution, but commercial fishermen and local and visiting divers as well. Interested divers can visit the laboratory, but on appointment only. Call the Discovery Bay Marine Lab at (809) 973-2241.

Depth Range:	70–110 ft (21–33 m)
Currents:	Moderate
Classification:	Advanced
Access:	Boat—mooring buoy

Another great wall dive, this one is a favorite of many dive operators of the area. It starts at 70 ft (21 m) where the bottom slopes down to 80 ft (24 m), after which the wall drops down to a sand shelf reaching more than 140 ft (42 m). As with many deep sites, the area is covered wth red deep-water gorgonians, elephant ear sponges in various colors, and a number of different basket and barrel sponges. The large branches of the sea plumes bend in the current and due to their pale color, may resemble a small, snow-covered tree. Large trumpetfish may hover beside a branch using them as camouflage. Rope sponges sometimes fuse with other sponges to form a multicolored structure. Barracudas roam the reef and spotted eagle rays are often seen.

The sand flat attracts Atlantic stingrays, whose presence, if you do not see them on the dive, can be observed from the large hollows they leave behind, after feeding on mollusks that are buried in the sand. Schools of small blue tropicals drift over the top of the reef and among the black feather coral, four-eye butterflyfish travel in pairs. Different species of large and small parrotfish feed on the algae and coral polyps, contributing to the sand that will eventually end up on the beaches. (According to Dr. William Alevizon, author of *Pisces Guide to Caribbean Reef Ecology,* an adult parrotfish ingests and excretes almost 1 ton of "coral sand" each year!)

The coral heads at times form crevices in which lobsters and king crabs can hide, but sometimes these nocturnal creatures venture out during the day. Swimming back to the mooring, groups of schoolmaster snappers can be seen drifting over the reef. During your safety stop, you may have the opportunity to watch some of the creatures that live near the ocean surface. Comb jellies, which do not have stinging cells, may swim by, giving you a chance to closely observe their delicate structure and jet-like motion. It is from animals like this one that creators of science fiction films might get their ideas.

Depth Range:	30 ft (9 m)
Currents:	None, sometimes wind-related swells
Classification:	Novice
Access:	Boat—anchor

This is a beautiful shallow reef, a favorite also for night diving. The dive-masters have been feeding the fish here, so you will find most of them quite tame. Remarkable are the large lane snappers, which allow the divers to come very close, before moving away. The reef area, bordering on a large

Chromis, parrotfish, soldierfish and damsels are plentiful at the beautiful reef of Silver Spray. ▶

◀ *A diver hovers behind a barrel sponge on which a red rope sponge resembles a giant starfish.*

There are an amazing number of sea fans at Silver Spray Reef.

sand flat, is virtually covered with sea fans, sea rods and sea plumes, sway-ing back and forth in the light swells. Pillar corals reach up towards the sur-face and clouds of brown chromis will part when a diver passes through.

When food comes out, the whole fish community gathers around the divers, and one may actually risk being bitten by the more aggressive sergeant majors. Even trumpetfish will join in the hope of catching some-thing and on a rare occasion will approach a diver to come in front of his mask for a closer look.

At night the other residents of the reef—the lobsters, crabs, and octo-puses—take their place and basket starfish climb up to the top of the sea fans and coral heads to spread out their arms. They, like the sea fans, feed on plankton, which is suspended in the water that flows by their tentacles and polyps.

Navigating through a reef with sea fans is always easy, because, in order to take advantage of the water flow, they are always positioned per-pendicular to the normal water flow and if a diver wants to swim in a cer-tain direction, he/she only has to keep the same angle in relation to the fans. The time of day and the position of the sun provide the additional clues to determine north-south and east-west direction.

6

Diving the Ocho Rios Area

Continuing on along the north coast road, the next area you get to is Ocho Rios. Spanish for "Eight Rivers," it indicates that there are quite a number of rivers emptying into this bay. Depending on the weather, this may have some influence on the visibility, but generally it is quite good, especially on the deeper sites.

The diving around Ocho Rios is divided into two areas, west of the bay and east of the bay, with most operators located at the east end. Most sites are near to shore, so the boat rides are pleasantly short around here. The reef shelf is quite narrow and the drop-off comes close to shore allowing easy access to great walls, covered with deep-water gorgonians and an

Visitors climb the Dunn's River Falls in Ocho Rios.

assortment of sponges. The shallow reefs have interesting coral formations, especially on the east side where there are caverns and sand channels in between the reef fingers that extend towards the deeper water. Nurse sharks are seen regularly at various locations.

There is a wide variety of after-dive activities in the area—climbing the famous Dunn's River Falls, sailing or windsurfing, parasailing, deep-sea fishing, touring a working plantation, horseback riding, or shopping in downtown Ocho Rios. Of course, you can also opt for a relaxing afternoon at the beach or the poolside, with a good book.

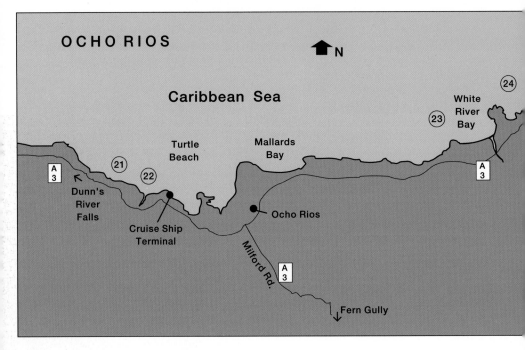

Dive Site Ratings	Novice	Intermediate	Advanced
Ocho Rios Area			
21 Jacks Hall	X	X	X
22 Top of the Mountain		X	X
23 Devils Reef			X
24 Wreck of the *Kathryn*—Caverns*	X	X	X

*This area offers excellent snorkeling also.

Depth Range:	30–50 ft (9–15 m).
Currents:	Light to medium, depending on the weather
Classification:	Novice
Access:	Boat—drift

Another good example of the spur and grove type reef structure is Jacks Hall. This medium-profile reef has finger coral, brain coral, star coral, an occasional elkhorn coral on the shallower end, and a variety of sponges. Drifting with the current you pass over a section of reef, followed by a sand chute, another reef section and another sand gully and so on. Nurse sharks frequent the area and can often be found napping in the sand, so there is always the expectation that you might see them in the next channel, or perhaps in the next one?

A large variety of coral species is visible on each side of this sandy gully at Jacks Hall.

The polyps of pillar coral are extended even during the day, giving the coral a soft spongy appearance from a distance.

If you have a keen eye, you may spot a scorpionfish, resembling a lumpy piece of coral, blending perfectly with the background of the reef. Sometimes two reef sections extend over the sand chute to form a small tunnel. Inside, lobsters and crabs hide together with the black long-spined sea urchins that have made a good comeback in this area. The West Indian sea egg, another type of sea urchin with short white spines, can also be seen. Due to these urchins, and the work of the doctorfish and parrotfish, the reef is relatively clean of algae. When you focus on the smaller creatures that inhabit the reef, you will find the bearded fire worm, definitely not something you want to play with! The white bristles that emerge when the worm is disturbed easily penetrate the skin, and the resulting pain and itch are not very pleasant. Less dangerous—but no less attractive—is the lettuce sea slug, which you may find here in a variety of colors, from pale white to bright blue.

Depth Range:	60–80 ft (18–24 m).
Currents:	Light
Classification:	Intermediate
Access:	Boat—drift

Near Dunn's River Falls, a massive underwater mountain plateau rises up from the sandy ocean floor to 60 ft (18 m) below the surface. The top of the reef is covered with many different species of soft gorgonians and small coral heads, consisting of sea rods, sea plumes, sea fans, brain coral, star coral, and clusters of smooth flower coral. Near the edge you will see some large colonies of grooved-blade sea whips, a type of soft gorgonian that is quite rare in Jamaica. In addition, you find small colonies of plate coral of an unusual reddish color that clearly stand out from their surroundings.

When you swim along the edge towards shallower water, look out for golden hamlets that frequent this area and the uncommon yellowcheek wrasse, otherwise only seen on the deeper dives in the Port Royal/Kingston area. Small barrel sponges dot the reef and green rope sponges wave in the mild current. When you look carefully, you may see the golden sponge zoanthids living on the surface of the rope sponges.

Friends of the Sea—Ocho Rios

In 1991, a group of concerned citizens from St. Ann, a parish that includes Discovery Bay, Runaway Bay, and Ocho Rios, started a movement to halt the destruction of the marine environment and the shoreline of the area. Calling themselves "Friends of the Sea," their objective is to increase the public awareness of this problem and to educate all levels of the society about it, from school children and the business community to public officials. Their newsletter *Seaview* does not limit itself to marine issues, but is a forum to point out positive solutions to environmental problems the citizens face. Besides educational programs, their projects include water quality monitoring and the introduction of re-usable canvas shopping bags, using local resources for production and marketing.

For more information about their activities you can write to: Friends of the Sea, P.O. Box 327, St. Ann's Bay—Jamaica W.I.

A diver is partially hidden behind this uncommon grooved-blade sea whip on Top of the Mountain.

Hiding in the coral heads are glasseye snappers, graysbys, and squir-relfish. In the shallow reef at about 50 ft (15 m) the area is sandy, with some low-profile hard coral, and you can see black-ball, orange-ball, and stinker sponges in between the small mounds of starlet coral. Besides all the regular damsels, indigo and shy hamlets move about in the company of rock beauties and redband parrotfish.

Depth Range:	65–90 ft (20–28 m)
Currents:	Variable, from none to strong, depending on the weather
Classification:	Advanced
Access:	Boat—anchor

Located east of Ocho Rios, Devils Reef is only a short boat ride away for most of the dive operators of the area. This underwater ridge, about ½ mile off-shore (¾ km) slopes down to about 65 feet (20 m) after which the wall drops down into very deep water. There is no mooring here, and because the currents are unpredictable, the dive boat will anchor in the sand at 60 ft. (18 m). From there the divemaster will lead you through a low profile reef with many black-ball sponges, green finger sponges, and

A colony of flower coral and red rope sponge create an interesting contrast on top of Devils Reef.

The large green moray at Devils Reef gets nervous from so much attention and prepares to withdraw in his hole.

patches of new staghorn growth to the edge of the drop-off, where you can look down at a sandy bottom at 120–130 ft (36–40 m). Down below, small groups of snapper swim around, but the main activity is around 70–80 ft (21–24 m). Schools of bogas and creole wrasse speed by and a school of Atlantic spadefish will tantalize you to come out into the deep water. Unfortunately for photographers, they stay too far away from the edge and the divers to get a good shot of them. The resident barracuda and the ceros that pass by also stay just outside of your strobe's reach.

Along the side of the ridge, however, there are plenty of photo opportunities; sponges in many colors abound and the big spread of the deep-water sea fans and large stands of black coral provide a great background for the blackbar soldierfish. On the top of the ridge are many small cracks and crevices and some overhangs providing protection for a variety of marine life. Large green moray eels move inside the coral heads and a closer look may reveal a spotted trunkfish or a juvenile tiger grouper. Over colonies of feather black coral, sunshinefish will school and the serious fish watcher may be able to spot the rare masked hamlet that resides at Devils Reef.

Depth Range:	20–50 ft (7–15 m)
Currents:	Tidal, if any
Classification:	Novice and snorkelers
Access:	Boat

Just north of a very pretty shallow reef, ideal for snorkelers, lies the wreck of the *Kathryn.* The 140-ft (43-m) steel-hulled ex-mine sweeper was deliberately sunk there by an Ocho Rios dive operator in 1991. It sits upright, with a slight list to starboard, in the middle of a large sandy area, which is covered with manatee grass and other algae at a depth of 50 ft (15 m). The superstructure is completely intact and allows easy entry to its interior, which is spacious enough to move around. Inside, due to the darkness, black coral, which is normally found much deeper, has started to grow, and the outside has already acquired patches of brain coral and a variety of sponges. Scattered over the surface you can also find large tunicates.

A squirrelfish looks on while a diver explores the side of the Kathryn.

Looking in through a porthole, a diver examines the growth inside the wreck of the Kathryn. Sponges and black coral are already starting to grow on it.

The wreck is host to many fish that find shelter and food in and on the vessel. Coneys and an occasional graysby gather at the keel and large groups of squirrelfish come to greet the divers. They are very curious and have obviously been fed, because whenever you stop somewhere for a closer look, they will surround you hoping for a free meal. Damsels, and specifically the sergeant majors, are busy defending their territory or guarding the purple egg-patches that are stuck to the hull. Amid this activity, yellow goatfish are digging in the sediment, parrotfish are nibbling at the vegetation, and Spanish hogfish add their purple and yellow to the colorful scenery. For a good look at the complete wreck, you need to gain some distance. Ascend to about 20 feet (7 m), move slightly away from it and you'll be rewarded with a great overview of the *Kathryn.*

Toward the shallow section, the reef is cut in deep trenches with the coral walls rising to just below the surface. This area is called "The Caverns," and is sometimes used as a separate dive site. Inside the caverns and ledges, glassy sweepers and lobsters are hiding, and on the sandy bottom you'll see the burrows of the sand tilefish, some tobaccofish, and the furry sea cucumber moving about. Nurse sharks are seen quite regularly. Toward the shallow end, huge elkhorn coral stands are the playground for many juvenile fish providing hours of fun and enjoyment for snorkelers and scuba divers alike. The more adventurous snorkeler can swim out to the wreck and free dive down to the top of the structure.

7

Diving the Port Antonio Area

Located far to the east on the northcoast of the island, about 4 hours from Montego Bay and 2 hours from Kingston, Port Antonio is still a secret among travelers. Nestled at the foot of the John Crow and Blue Mountains, the scenery is breathtaking. Although many local divers from the Kingston area dive there, not many tourist divers have discovered this destination. Because of the impact that hurricane Allen, which passed through in 1980, had on the shallow reefs, you will find the best sites in deep water. These are excellent, and offer a variety of marine life and underwater scenery. Some critters that are rare at other sites around the island, like the black and white crinoid and the porkfish, can be observed here. Several dive sites have been named after a large rock formation at the shoreline, which resembles the head of an alligator, resulting in names like Alligator Head, Alligator Long, and Alligator Deep.

A panorama of Blue Hole and the coastline of Port Antonio.

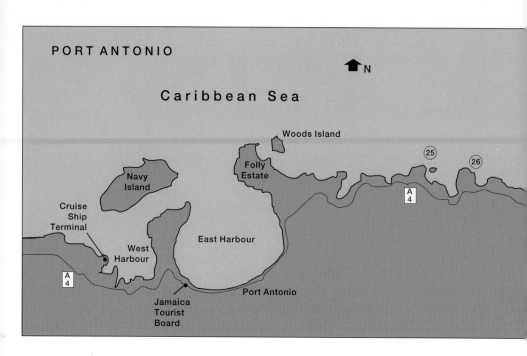

Dive Site Ratings

	Novice	Intermediate	Advanced
Port Antonio Area			
25 Alligator Long			X
26 Dragon Bay	X	X	X

The shallow reefs show signs of recovery and provide ample opportunity for divers as well as snorkelers for fish watching, and many invertebrates can be found if you take the time to look for them. And, of course, for the after-dive hours there is rafting on the Rio Grande, discovering caves at Non-Such, or simply cooling off in the waterfalls at Reach. Don't leave without sampling the original "jerk" pork or chicken, a hot and spicy delicacy barbecued on a special grill at Boston Beach, located only a couple of miles east of Port Antonio.

Depth Range:	80–90 ft (24–27 m)
Currents:	Light
Classification:	Advanced
Access:	Boat—drift dive

After being dropped off by the boat, which will follow the divers, a free descent leads to a narrow coral ridge, rising 20 to 30 ft (7–9 m) from a large sand flat at 100 ft (30 m). You follow the ridge in an easterly direction, drifting along on the mostly gentle current. This ridge is a fantastic dive site, but beware: It is easy to become absorbed in the sights, and your time at that depth is limited.

The top of the ridge is covered with soft gorgonians, sea fans, all types of sponges, including large basket sponges, and an abundance of healthy coral heads. In between you will see golden crinoids, and with some luck you may see the black and white crinoid on top of a basket sponge or fan. Their tentacles are spread out in all directions to catch the minute particles, suspended in the water, on which they feed. When you look towards the center, where the mouth is located, the black tentacles with the white accents create an intricate geometric pattern.

Some porkfish, and a variety of hamlets such as the butter hamlet, the barred and the indigo hamlet are all around. Squirrelfish are seen between the sponges and the coral heads and bi-color damsels dart back and forth. Along the sides of the ridge, elephant ear sponges compete for space with red deep-water sea fans. Cruising the sand flat are stingrays, black durgeons, and Atlantic triggerfish; spadefish are common visitors at this site.

A close-up look at the top of an azure vase sponge, quite common on the reefs in Jamaica.

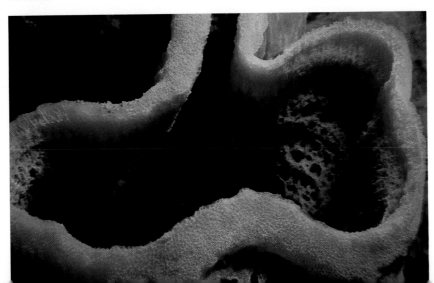

A basket sponge and a variety of other sponges on the ridge of Alligator Long.

Dragon Bay 26

Depth Range:	30–65 ft (9–20 m)
Currents:	Light
Classification:	Novice
Access:	Boat—drift dive

Patches of healthy staghorn coral are spreading out over the remains of older coral structures that collapsed during storms, in this shallow reef. Sloping down, the reef forms finger-like structures with sandy areas in between, ending on a deeper sand flat. What is remarkable about this reef is the abundance of golden crinoids; wherever you look there is one, sticking its tentacles out from the coral heads. Of course, the brown, beaded variety is also present. Looking carefully you may see peacock flounders gliding over rounded coral heads, changing their colors rapidly to blend in with the background. Coneys in two color patterns, blue chromis, rock

Golden crinoids can be found in large numbers at the shallow reef in Dragon Bay.

A four-eye butterflyfish looking for food near a colony of star coral (Photograph courtesy of Terry Silsbury).

beauties, and sand divers also inhabit this reef. You may notice a rock beauty or blackbar soldier fish swimming around with something that resembles a big bug attached to its head. The "bug" is an isopod that attaches to its host to get free meals. The one that you see is most often a female, while the much smaller male can be found elsewhere on the body of the fish. In Jamaica they are called the "cockroach of the sea."

In this reef we discovered a new species or color variation of hamlet we have not seen mentioned in fish identification books. It has the markings of a three-spot damsel with a tan coloring and a black spot on the snout, and yes, of course, it eluded the photographer! Experts are still debating the possibility of interbreeding between the different hamlets, but the number of hamlets with uncommon color patterns that can be seen around Jamaica would give credit to that theory.

A fair amount of soft gorgonians and sea fans can be seen. If you look close you may even find a fringed filefish hiding among the branches. In the reef area nearby, nurse sharks can be seen regularly and sometimes they will pass through this reef.

8

Diving the Port Royal/Kingston Area

Kingston, the capital of Jamaica, has only recently started to market itself as a tourist destination. Some of the attractions here are the old buildings from the colonial days and of course the remains of Port Royal, now mainly submerged after it was destroyed in 1692 by an earthquake and following tidal wave. Underwater archeologists have used this site to research life in the 1600s, as the sunken city still harbors many artifacts from that period. Because of this, up to the day of writing, recreational divers are not allowed to dive the site. Regardless, its proximity to Kingston Harbor, with the resulting low visibility and boats passing overhead, makes this a dive for experienced divers.

Cannons at Port Royal are a reminder of the tumultuous years of the past.

Local divers from the Jamaica Sub Aqua Club and the University Sub Aqua Club have in the past dived sites near the harbor and found most of them disappointing at best. Only in the last couple of years have other reefs farther off shore been explored and some great sites discovered near the Cays. Because of the geographical location and common wind direction, diving is mainly done in the early morning, which provides the calmest seas and best visibility. During the winter months, on days when diving on the north coast must be canceled due to a "northern", the Port Royal area is on the lee side and you can still get a couple of good dives in. Trips are also organized to the nearby mangroves, providing an opportunity to watch pelicans, frigate birds, and egrets, and if you are lucky you may even encounter a pod of dolphins.

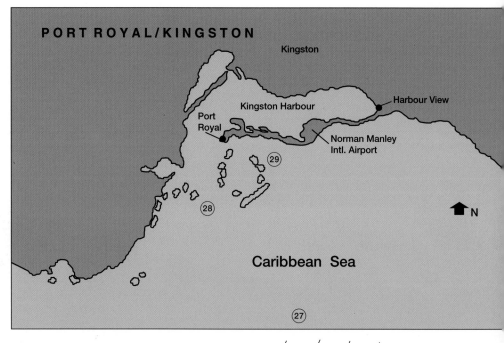

Dive Site Ratings	Novice	Intermediate	Advanced
Port Royal/Kingston Area			
27 Windward Edge			X
28 Wreck of the *Cayman Trader*	X	X	X
29 Southeast Cay Wall		X	X

Depth Range:	70–90 ft (21–28 m)
Currents:	Light
Classification:	Advanced
Access:	Boat—drift

Located about 7 miles outside of the Kingston Cays, this site takes a 20-minute boat ride on a fast, rigid keel inflatable to get there, and because it can get quite windy and choppy later during the day, this dive is always planned in the early morning. However, the dive is definitely worth it. This is truly a blue water dive. On days that the seas are calm, the visibility is 100 ft (30 m) plus, and the clarity and color of the water are unbelievable. The distance from shore prevents possible pollution and sedimentation, and the condition of the reef is pristine with hardly any algae growth.

Making a free descent, you can see the reef lying 70 feet (21 m) below you, and the gentle current sways the soft gorgonians that are plentiful on this site. Basically a low-profile reef, it slopes from 60 feet (18 m) to about 100 feet (30 m) and beyond the edge it drops to more than 1,000 feet (300 m). The bottom is covered with small coral heads, sea rods, sea plumes and sea

The variety of coral and the clear, deep blue water make this deep dive special.

A diver floats over a very healthy stand of staghorn coral at Windward Edge.

fans, and some feather black coral. Swimming in between all this are schools of chromis, creole wrasse, redband and striped parrotfish. Bluehead wrasse, yellowhead wrasse, and yellowcheek wrasse are abundant here. Actually, we had only seen the yellowcheek wrasse once before on the north coast of Jamaica. For a touch of color there are azure vase sponges; orange, red, and purple rope sponges; yellow and purple tube sponges; and some black ball sponges. You should look inside the clusters of smooth star coral and brain coral; peeking out are golden crinoids, spotted moray eels, and above it you can observe black durgeons drifting along. Our guide had told us that in the last months they have had numerous encounters with dolphins at this site, and we had watched a video taken on one of those occasions. We did not see any that day, but when it happens it must be an awesome experience.

Towards the shallower side of the reef there are new, big healthy stands of staghorn coral attracting myriad juvenile fish. Unfortunately, the bottom time on these dives is always too short to really explore it all, but on the free swimming safety stop (check your depth gauge or computer regularly!) you can look down for a last view on one of the most untouched reefs in Jamaica.

86

Depth Range:	30–50 ft (9–15 m)
Currents:	Light, inside wreck surges
Classification:	Novice
Access:	Boat—mooring

One of the wrecks that can be dived out of Port Royal is that of the *Cayman Trader*. This cargo ship, originally built in 1950 in Norway, and later lengthened to nearly 300 ft (90 m) long, was in the Kingston harbor with a load of lumber in August of 1977 when it caught fire. The fire tender that came to its assistance used a large amount of water to put out the blaze, which caused the vessel to list. After several months in the harbor it had taken in so much water that the authorities were afraid that it might sink right there, so the decision was made to tow it to deep water and sink it. As fate would have it, on the way out, the tow line broke and the burnt-out cargo ship was washed up onto the South East Reef. There it remained with most of its superstructure above water, the bow wedged on the reef and the stern in about 50 ft (15m) of water. The next year's storms and wave action caused the vessel to break up, and when it was finally completely submerged, it became a popular dive site.

Now the wreck is scattered over a large area, but several parts of it are easily identified, from the bow section in shallow water to the large bronze propeller lying in the sand separate from the wreck. In the years

A permanent resident of the Cayman Trader, *this trumpetfish observes the intruder exploring the wreck.*

gone by, coral and other marine organisms have started to cover the wreck and large patches of brain coral can be found everywhere on the flat surfaces. Inside, the crevices of the wreck provide hiding places for schools of glassy sweepers, juvenile grunts, Spanish hogfish, saddled blennies, soldierfish, and the occasional green moray and large parrotfish. Crawling about there are bristleworms, and if you look closely you can even spot some tubastraea, the orange cup coral.

Novice divers should not enter the more enclosed areas because a sometimes quite heavy surge can throw the unsuspecting diver about, causing possible injury on sharp edges. While swimming around the wreck, look out for sergeant majors swimming back and forth along the hull, which become very excited when you approach them. These are the males, busily guarding the purple egg patches you can see behind them on the metal panels of the wreck. In the area immediately around the wreck, you can see barracuda, puddingwifes, yellowtail snapper, porkfish, doctorfish, blue tangs, and the occasional Spanish grunt. Spread out over the sandy area in 50 ft (15m) are some small coral heads in which squirrelfish, blackbar soldierfish, and sometimes a porcupinefish hide. Southern stingrays and Bermuda chubs are also common visitors.

In the shallow reef, storms and hurricanes have done a lot of damage to the coral formations, but it is encouraging to see new stands of staghorn and elkhorn coral. Take some time to look around; nurse sharks and barracuda are seen quite regularly, and on one dive a spotted eagle ray came flying by.

A diver is silhouetted against the sun while ascending from the Cayman Trader.

Depth Range:	30–90 ft (9–28 m)
Currents:	Light
Classification:	Intermediate
Access:	Boat—drift

Normally done as a drift dive, this site features a multilevel profile. After descending to the top of the drop-off at 50 feet (15 m), the wall goes down to a sand flat at about 90 feet (28 m). The crevices on this wall, formed by plate coral, are perfect hiding places for all kinds of invertebrates, and even if the visibility of this site is not like that of those farther offshore, there is still plenty to see during the 45 to 60 minutes that are normally spent here. It is advisable to bring a dive light to discover the creatures that hide in the darker recesses of the overhangs. Queen angels can be seen, and of course the fairy basslets that like to swim upside down under the ceiling of the crevices.

Following the wall in an easterly direction, you'll see antennae poking out from under a ledge, and a closer look reveals spiny lobsters, or the more colorful but smaller rock lobster. Scurrying about we saw a king

A spiny lobster at East Cay wall is caught by the photographer in bright daylight.

A big-eye snapper standing before his usual hiding place, a ledge covered with sponges. Note the orange cup coral at the right hand top of the photograph!

crab waving his hand-sized claws at us before retreating into the dark hole in which he normally hides during the day. You should not forget to look down towards the sand or up to the edge of the reef, as ceros (called king-fish in Jamaica) can be seen passing by, as are individual Spanish and Caesar grunts. In the sand there are always some yellow goatfish digging around for food along with tobaccofish. Over the sand are seen the lane snapper, looking very much like a grunt, but with a black dot towards the tail, and some yellowtail snappers going about their business.

Gradually, the sand flat comes up, and after about 25 minutes the dive continues in the shallow reef. Continuing towards the east, the reef slowly rises from 50 feet (15 m) to 30 feet (9 m) creating a nice gradual ascent. This reef, much closer to shore than Windward Edge, has been exposed to the forces of nature, and the hurricanes of the last two decades have taken their toll. The shallow, spur-and-groove type reef shows signs of storm damage. But there are signs of recovery, new staghorn coral is growing among the more sturdy and storm resistant brain coral, but most of the sea fans look rather frayed. The reef has more profile, and in the sandy areas between the coral heads you can see parrotfish, rock beauties, bar jacks, damsels, and many types of wrasse. Nurse sharks are also quite common here, resting or moving through the gullies that are formed by the sand in between the coral.

9

Snorkeling Around the Island

Snorkeling is an activity that one can do with the whole family, regardless of the age of the members, and for that reason, among others, it enjoys increasing popularity. Also, you only need a limited amount of gear, easy to bring along wherever you go, to explore the world below the surface, and quite often you do not even need a boat. Sometimes the best place to watch the marine life of an area is from the surface, and they go about their business as if you are not there.

In Jamaica there are many sites near shore that are suitable for snorkeling, but not too many are easily accessible. There is either a very shallow impassable reef crest between you and where you want to go, or the swim out to the reef is through an area that has heavy boat traffic, making it quite dangerous. Some of the public beaches that are away from the resort areas would be the best bet to snorkel from shore. One word of advice: watch the weather, ask locals for information before you go in, accept your own limitations, and do not take any risks. Those locations are also a fair distance from any medical facility and assistance, if you would need any!

Booby Cay in Negril is a popular site for snorkeling trips.

These snorkelers are enjoying the shallow reef near the Kathryn in Ocho Rios.

In all resort areas, however, you will find watersport operators offering trips, some of them guided, out to the reefs. Make sure you only go with an operator licensed by the Jamaica Tourist Board, because those are the ones that comply with all the safety regulations.

Several dive operators also offer snorkeling lessons for those who are new to it, and snorkel trips, sometimes in combination with divers at one of their shallow sites. If the mooring is at less than 30 ft (9m) you will have a good chance of getting close enough to the reef to get a good look. Some of the sites that are used for that, and are described in this book, are sites number 8 (the Classroom area), 9, 15, 20 (the shallow side), and 24. In addition to that, the Westend in Negril also provides you with possibilities for shore entry. Check with the dive operators in that area where the easiest entry is.

Crocodiles and Manatees

The crest on the Jamaican coat of arms features a crocodile, one of the largest wild animals in Jamaica and also one of the largest reptiles in the world. There is very little chance to encounter them, unless you dive or snorkel in one of the many rivers on the south coast. Touring the island and perhaps taking a trip up the Black River (about a one-and-a-half-hour drive from Montego Bay and Negril) to see the wetlands and mangroves, you may observe them basking in the sun on the river bank, or passing by in the late afternoon searching for a meal. Although there are many of them left in the wetlands of the south coast, crocodiles are on the endangered species list in Jamaica and therefore protected by law.

Also on the endangered species list is the West Indian manatee, in Jamaica called "sea cow." There are no exact counts of how many manatees there actually are, but most estimates do not exceed one hundred of these mammals, which live mainly in rivers and brackish areas near a freshwater source, like a spring. In Jamaica you can find them on the south coast, and one area in particular, Canoe Valley, offers a reasonably good chance to observe them. As part of the enforcement of the law, over the years four manatees were confiscated from fishermen, and placed in the Alligator Hole river for educational and research purposes. There is a small visitor center providing information about the animals in and around the river and on weekdays you may find a warden to take you on a boat tour.

A lazy crocodile is sunning on the banks of a pond.

10

Responsible and Safe Diving

Protection of the Marine Environment

As you may have read earlier on in this guide, Jamaica and the dive operators are trying to protect the marine environment and the dive sites that give so much pleasure to divers, locals, and visitors alike. They will need your help to control one of the factors that influence reef degradation: diver damage. Establishing mooring buoys is not enough; all divers should become aware of the impact they can have on reefs. An uncontrolled descent can cause sediment to be kicked up onto the coral, thereby smothering it. An over-weighted diver who must hold on to something to steady him/herself, will cause damage, and the photographer, in his/her quest for another great shot, can destroy the marine life under or behind him/her. It takes only seconds to destroy something that take years, or decades, to grow.

On the other hand, it also takes very little to minimize the effects of our interaction with the marine environment. Some preparation before the dive, a little knowledge about the creatures you are about to encounter, and the proper dive skills are all that is necessary to ensure that the divers following you can enjoy it, too.

The recompression chamber of the Discovery Bay Marine Laboratory is always on stand-by for emergencies.

Following is a list of tips for protecting our dive sites, not only for those who are new to warm water, coral reef diving, but also as a reminder for the more experienced diver whose diving may have become a bit too nonchalant.

Buoyancy Control. If you have never dived in warm water before, remember that you will need less thermal protection; in the summer you might even dive without a suit, and therefore you need less weight! If you are unsure about the amount you will need, follow the advice of the divemaster. Before descending do a buoyancy check—if you cannot go down with a deflated BCD you can always add a pound or two. Then, underwater, establish neutral buoyancy, so that you can hover if you want to look at something or take a photograph, instead of having to kick your fins to stay there. With proper buoyancy control you will also be able to experience that exhilarating feeling of being totally weightless, and you'll be rewarded with a reduction of your air consumption.

Don't Touch. There are many ways divers can cause damage to the reef. One is the careless kicking of your fins while in a vertical position. Try to make your descent onto a sandy area and establish neutral buoyancy before reaching the bottom to avoid kicking up sediment or damaging the coral. When swimming over sand or through tunnels, make sure to be in a horizontal position and far enough away from the bottom; not only will that prevent you from rising to the surface, but it will also give the divers following you the opportunity to enjoy the dive as well. If at any time you need to stabilize yourself by holding on to something, try and find a spot without growth on it, and do not use your whole hand, a finger will do. Remember your gauge consoles and octopus regulators: Don't drag them through the reef, but tuck them into your BCD or keep them close to your body.

Don't Harass the Animals. The time has passed when it was "good fun" to grab a balloonfish (pufferfish) and see it blow up in pure fright about what was happening to him. Have respect for the underwater creatures whose world you are temporarily sharing and do not go chasing after them or bothering them in any way. You will have more luck getting close to them if you are prepared to be patient and wait for them to approach you.

Pick Up the Trash. It can happen that, while diving, you see something that does not belong there—bottles, cans, or plastic cups that are discarded by careless boaters or beach visitors. Do your part to keep the reef clean and healthy; pick it up and if you do not have a pocket to temporarily store it until after the dive, give it to the divemaster. He or she will be happy to take care of it.

Learn About the Reef Inhabitants. It is easier to be careful if you know what you are looking at. Look through books that will help you to identify the individual species of fish, coral and invertebrates, and start your own list of critters you have seen while diving. Being more aware of your surroundings will also increase the fun you have on a dive!

Your Safety

Although all of the dives in Jamaica are guided dives, and no tanks are rented to visitors for unsupervised diving, as a certified diver you are still responsible for your own safety. If you bring your own equipment, make sure it is in good working order before starting your trip; if it is new, try it out in a pool first and bring some spare parts like a mask strap or fin straps. If you rent equipment that is unfamiliar to you, get accustomed to it, and make sure everything is functioning properly before boarding the dive boat.

If you have not been diving for some time, take a refresher course before you go on your holiday, and if you are new to coral reefs, you may want to take an orientation dive with one of the local dive operators. Although government regulations do not allow decompression dives, it is also your responsibility to maintain the maximum depth and time limit set by the divemaster for the dive. Bring your dive tables along and if you use a computer, don't push the limits. You will find that you have more time to enjoy your dive when you stay a bit shallower, instead of going for the maximum depth possible.

Potentially Hazardous Marine Life

Most marine animals you will encounter in Jamaican waters are not really dangerous; in fact, we tend to pose a greater danger to them than they do to us. One general rule you should keep in mind: If you don't bother them, they won't bother you. If you maintain proper buoyancy control and avoid touching the coral and other creatures, then you and they will be safe. However, sometimes even the best of intentions can misfire and accidents do happen. Some creatures cause only minor injuries, others could be potentially dangerous, requiring medical attention. To prevent possible mishaps, a list follows of those animals you should try to avoid:

Sea Urchins. After a virus killed nearly all black spiny sea urchins in the early eighties, they have made a slow comeback. Whereas they may be absent in some places, there can be an abundance of them at another location. This urchin, together with the West Indian sea egg, which can be found in seagrass beds, is responsible for most of the urchin injuries. The brittle spines easily penetrate the skin, even through gloves or wetsuit, and have little barbs, which prevent them from being extracted in one piece. It is best not to try to remove the spines yourself, because this can cause further infection. Because the spines are calcium-based, it sometimes helps to soak the affected area in vinegar or ammonia (yes, in urgent circumstances urine can do the job, too!) to assist the body in dissolving them. Afterwards an antibiotic cream can be applied. In a serious case or if infection occurs, a doctor should be consulted.

Fire Coral. On nearly every reef you can find fire coral. A creamy tan in color, it comes in a variety of shapes and because it can overgrow other coral, for example sea fans, it is not always easy to distinguish. Upon contact, the nematocysts, small stinging cells located on the polyps will discharge, causing a burning sensation of the skin. Rubbing the area will only induce further discharge, making it worse. After the dive apply some meat tenderizer to reduce the sting. An antibiotic or cortisone cream might be beneficial.

Hydroids. There are a variety of hydroids on the reefs, all causing a mild to moderate sting when touched. They can be found at any depth, but the most common place where divers get into problems with them is at mooring lines. The Christmas tree hydroid, a feathery structure with a single white polyp forming a little ball at the end of the branches, is one of the creatures that attach themselves onto mooring lines and divers, while descending or ascending, will find it difficult to avoid. Because hydroids

Hydroids, growing on mooring lines, can cause a nasty burning sensation on your hands when touched.

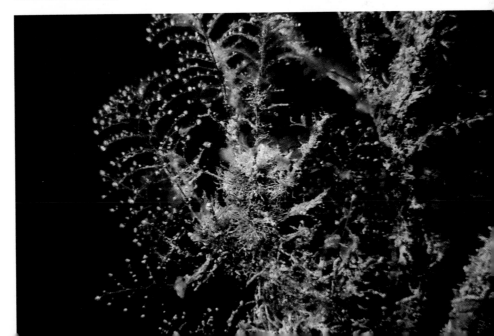

belong to the same class as fire coral, first aid for stings is the same: application of meat tenderizer and cortisone cream.

Fire or Bristleworms. This worm, resembling a large centipede, can be seen crawling through the reef, feeding on polyps of staghorn coral and soft gorgonians. Don't play with them; the bristles of white hair that become visible when the worm is disturbed will penetrate your skin and are nearly impossible to remove. They will cause an irritation that can last a few days and is quite painful. Cortisone cream may help to ease the pain.

Sea Wasps and Other Jellyfish. Sea wasps can pose a serious danger to divers, particularly at night. This very toxic member of the box jelly family resembles a small, square open box with one tentacle on each of the four corners. The length of the body is between 1 and 3 inches (2.5-7.5 cm), but the size is not indicative of the sting they can produce. Generally, they are translucent and seen mainly at night when they are attracted to light and come towards the surface. They can appear in large swarms and sometimes it is impossible to avoid them. One way to avoid being stung is to always wear full protective clothing when night diving—wetsuit or wetskin, boots and gloves, and, if available, a hood covering the face, leaving a space only for the regulator and mask. When you do get stung, abort the dive, do not rub to prevent further discharge, and flush the area with vinegar. Severe stings, especially in the face and throat area, may cause breathing difficulty and shock in susceptible divers. Provide first aid and seek immediate medical attention.

Depending on the time of the year, you may see other types of box jellies floating near the surface. Most of them do not sting, but in between may be others that do. Again, vinegar can be used to flush the area and in certain cases, where an allergic reaction occurred that did not get relief after treatment with cortisone, we have had good results with an acne medication containing benzoyl peroxide. As to the larger jellyfish like moon jellies or Portuguese man-of-war, they are easily seen from a distance, and contact can be avoided.

Sponges. Some of the beautifully colored sponges can also produce a mild sting, but if you follow the "hands off" rule, that type of injury is rare. Vinegar and meat tenderizer can be used as first aid, followed with a cortisone cream.

Stingrays. Although southern and yellow stingrays are able to cause a potential serious injury with their venomous spine located at the base of the tail, they will not seek you out to do so. If you do not disturb them when they lie in the sand, and shuffle your feet when entering the water from shore, you can avoid the sting. If it still has happened, seek medical attention as soon as possible, but if there is a time delay, it helps to keep the injured area submerged in water, as hot as you can tolerate. This will assist in breaking down the protein-based venom and alleviates the pain.

Scorpionfish. Sometimes these are also called stonefish or, by Jamaicans, "poisonous grouper." Like the rays, these fish have spines, containing a venom, which is used as a defense against possible attackers. Scorpionfish are experts in camouflage and blend in very well with their background. They will tend to lie motionless unless seriously harassed, after which they will quickly move away. If, by chance, you do get stung, first aid and treatment is the same as mentioned above for stingray punctures.

Barracudas. Although their appearance is intimidating, they are not really dangerous animals. Because they need to pump water through their gills to breath, they are often seen with their mouth open, displaying a fierce set of teeth. However, these are normally not used on humans, providing you follow the basic rule of leaving them alone. In stand-off situations where a barracuda approaches you, don't swim away but swim towards him. They are generally the losers in this game and will turn away from you. As a photographer, you will rarely come into that situation, because they are extremely camera-shy and will keep their distance!

Moray Eels. Moray eels, like barracudas, are not as bad as their reputation. It is wise not to feed them, because it may change the behavior of these normally shy creatures. Also their eyesight is not all that good, and they may be unable to distinguish between your hand and the food that you brought. Another possibility for a moray eel bite occurs when you put

Look, but don't touch. A scorpionfish lies well camouflaged between the algae.

your hands into crevices you cannot look into. If a moray eel resides there, it will naturally defend its home, to your detriment. If you do get bitten, try not to pull your hand away, but let the eel release you voluntarily to prevent further tearing of the wound. Ascend, apply first aid, and seek medical attention.

Sharks. Besides the normally docile nurse sharks, it is rare to see a shark while diving in Jamaica. If you do see one, remain calm and do not head for the surface. Just admire their sleek beauty and wait for them to leave the area before moving on. Generally, sharks seen here are not aggressive and there have been no reports of shark attacks on divers. Although the nurse sharks that can be seen regularly are, as a rule, harmless, you should not harass them. They still are pretty big animals with strong tails and jaws, enough so to get you into trouble. Besides, if they feel stressed, you or other divers may never see them at that spot again.

Diving Accidents

Although diving is a very safe sport and even if every precaution is being taken by a dive operation, the divemaster, and the divers involved, accidents do happen, although not very often, and you should know what to do, just in case. The dive operations that are licensed by the Jamaica Tourist Board are all well equipped to deal with an emergency. All boat crew and divemasters are trained in CPR and first aid, and there is oxygen on board every dive boat. Most boats have VHF radio to alert the facility that there is a problem, so that preparations can be started while the diver is being brought back to shore. Because very few doctors and hospitals in Jamaica are familiar with the specific problems associated with diving accidents, it is best to immediately contact the safety officer at the recompression chamber located at the Discovery Bay Marine Laboratory. He will arrange for air transport where required and will advise about the procedure to be followed. He is also able to contact DAN (Divers Alert Network) for consultation where necessary.

Hyperbaric treatment and air ambulance can be very costly, but if your own medical insurance does not cover it, there are specific insurance policies available for this purpose. Contact your local dive shop or DAN for more information.

Important Phone Numbers:
Emergency—Police: 119
Recompression chamber in Discovery Bay (0) 973-3274 (24 hours)
or from 9:00 am to 5:00 pm (0) 973-2241
Divers Alert Network (919) 684-8111 (Emergencies only)
Divers Alert Network (919) 684-2948 information

Appendix: Diving Operations

The list below is included as a service to the reader and is as accurate as possible at the time of printing. This list does not constitute an endorsement of these facilities. If operators/owners wish to be included in future reprints/editions, please contact Pisces Books, P.O. Box 2608, Houston, Texas 77252-2608, USA.

Negril Area

Blue Whale Divers
P.O. Box 83
Negril, Jamaica W.I.
Phone/Fax: (809) 957-4438

Grand Lido Hotel
P.O. Box 88
Negril, Jamaica W.I.
Phone: (809) 957-4010 to 4
Fax: (809) 957-4317

Dolphin Divers
P.O. Box 104
Negril, Jamaica W.I
Phone: (809) 957-4944
Fax: (809) 957-4849

Hedonism II
P.O. Box 25
Negril, Jamaica W.I.
Phone: (809) 957-4200
Fax: (809) 957-4289

Mariners Inn
P.O. Box 16
Negril, Jamaica W.I.
Phone: (809) 957-4348 or 4474
Fax: (809) 957-4472

Negril Scuba Centre
P.O. Box 49
Negril, Jamaica W.I.
Phone: 1-800-818-2963 or
(809) 957-4425
Fax: (809) 957-4425

Oli's Watersport
Negril P.O.
Negril, Jamaica W.I.
Phone: (809) 957-4300 or
(809) 997-5392
Fax: (809) 957-4301

Resort Divers—Negril
c/o P.O. Box 58
Runaway Bay, Jamaica W.I.
Phone: (809) 974-5338
Fax: (809) 974-0577

Sandals—Negril
c/o Sandals Resorts
P.O. Box 100
Montego Bay, Jamaica W.I.
Phone: 1-800-SANDALS or
(809) 979-9130 to 3
Fax: (809) 979-0556

Scuba World
Negril Cabins
P.O. Box 118
Negril, Jamaica W.I.
Phone/Fax: (809) 957-6290

Sundivers—Negril
c/o Poinciana Beach Hotel
Negril P.O.
Negril, Jamaica W.I.
Phone/Fax: (809) 957-4069

Westpoint Watersports
c/o Point Village Hotel
Negril P.O.
Negril, Jamaica W.I.
Phone: (809) 957-9170 to 9 ext. 364
Fax: (809) 957-6116

Montego Bay Area

Fun Divers
c/o Wyndham Rosehall
P.O. Box 999
Montego Bay, Jamaica W.I.
Phone/Fax : (809) 952-8299

Jamaica Rose Divers
White Sands Beach P.O.
Montego Bay, Jamaica W.I.
Phone /Fax: (809) 953-2714

Jamaica Scuba Divers
c/o North Coast Marine Sport
Greenwood P.O.
St. James, Jamaica W.I.
Phone/Fax: (809) 953-9266

Poseidon Divers
P.O. Box 152
Reading/St. James, Jamaica W.I.
Phone: 1-800-880-5224 or
(809) 952-3624
Fax: (809) 952-3079

Reef Keepers
P.O. Box 1427
Montego Bay, Jamaica W.I.
Phone: (809) 979-0102 to 4
Fax: (809) 979-0101

Resort Divers—Montego Bay
Shop # 8, Montego Bay Shopping
Centre
Howard Cooke Blvd.
Montego Bay, Jamaica W.I.
Phone: (809) 952-4258
Fax: (809) 952-4288

Sandals—Montego Bay
c/o Sandals Resorts
P.O. Box 100
Montego Bay, Jamaica W.I.
Phone: 1-800-SANDALS or
(809) 979-9130 to 3
Fax: (809) 979-0556

Scuba Connection
P.O. Box 300
Montego Bay, Jamaica W.I.
Phone: (809) 952-4780
Fax: (809) 952-7543

Seaworld Resort
P.O. Box 610
Montego Bay, Jamaica W.I.
Phone: (809) 953-2180
Fax: (809) 953-2550

Watersports Fantasy
c/o Tryall Golf, Tennis and Beach
Resort
P.O. Box 1206
Montego Bay, Jamaica W.I.
Phone: (809) 956-5660
Fax: (809) 956-5673

Runaway Bay Area

Jamaqua
c/o Club Caribbean
P.O. Box 65
Runaway Bay, Jamaica W.I.
Phone: (809) 973-4845
Fax: (809) 973-4875

Sundivers—Runaway Bay
P.O. Box 212
Runaway Bay, Jamaica W.I.
Phone: (809) 973-2346
Fax: (809) 973-2067

Resort Divers—Runaway Bay
c/o P.O. Box 58
Runaway Bay, Jamaica W.I.
Phone: (809) 974-5338
Fax: (809) 974-0577

Ocho Rios Area

Couples Hotel
P.O. Box 330
Ocho Rios, St. Ann, Jamaica W.I.

Phone: (809) 975-4271 to 5
Fax: (809) 975-4435

Fantasea Divers
c/o Boscobel Beach Hotel
P.O. Box 63
Ocho Rios, Jamaica W.I.
Phone: (809) 975-4504
Fax: (809) 975-7370

Garfield Diving Station
P.O. Box 394
Ocho Rios, Jamaica W.I.
Phone/Fax: (809) 974-5749

Island Divers
c/o La Mer Dive & Beach Resort
Tower Isle, St. Mary, Jamaica W.I.
Phone: (809) 975-5002 to 4
Fax: (809) 974-4341

P.R. Scuba Technologies
P.O. Box 327
St. Ann's Bay, St. Ann, Jamaica W.I.
Phone: (809) 974-1880
Fax: (809) 974-5428

Resort Divers—Ocho Rios
c/o P.O. Box 58
Runaway Bay, Jamaica W.I.
Phone: (809) 974-5338
Fax: (809) 974-0577

Sandals—Dunn's River, Ocho Rios
c/o Sandals Resorts
P.O. Box 100

Montego Bay, Jamaica W.I.
Phone: 1-800-SANDALS or
(809) 979-9130 to3
Fax: (809) 979-0556

Sea and Dive Jamaica
74 Main Street
Ocho Rios, Jamaica W.I.
Phone/Fax: (809) 974-5762

Watersports Enterprises
Arawak P.O.
St. Ann, Jamaica W.I.
Phone: (809) 974-2200 to 9
Fax: (809) 974-2185

Port Antonio Area

Aqua Action
2 Somerset Rd.
P.O. Box 81
Port Antonio
Phone: (809) 993-3426
Fax: (809) 993-3393

Kingston Area

Buccaneer Scuba Club
c/o Morgan's Harbour
Port Royal Kingston
Phone: (809) 924-8148
Fax: (809) 924-8146

The silhouette of a diver against the sun over a large colony of sea plumes.

Index

The **bold** printed page numbers indicate a photograph.

 **Pisces Books®**

Be sure to check out these other great books from Pisces:

Caribbean Reef Ecology
Great Reefs of the World
Skin Diver Magazine's Book of Fishes, 2nd Edition
Shooting Underwater Video: A Complete Guide to the Equipment and Techniques for
    Shooting, Editing, and Post-Production
Snorkeling . . . Here's How
Watching Fishes: Understanding Coral Reef Fish Behavior
Watersports Guide to Cancun

Diving and Snorkeling Guides to:

Australia: Coral Sea and Great Barrier Reef
Australia: Southeast Coast and Tasmania
The Bahamas: Family Islands and Grand
    Bahama
The Bahamas: Nassau and New Providence
    Island, 2nd Ed.
Bali
Belize
The Best Caribbean Diving
Bonaire
The British Virgin Islands
California's Central Coast
The Cayman Islands, 2nd Ed.
Cozumel, 2nd Ed.
Curaçao
Fiji
Florida's East Coast, 2nd Ed.
The Florida Keys, 2nd Ed.
The Great Lakes
Guam and Yap
The Hawaiian Islands, 2nd Ed.
Jamaica
Northern California and the Monterey
    Peninsula, 2nd Ed.
The Pacific Northwest
Palau
Puerto Rico
The Red Sea
Roatan and Honduras' Bay Islands
St. Maarten, Saba, and St. Eustatius
Southern California, 2nd Ed.
Texas
Truk Lagoon
The Turks and Caicos Islands
The U.S. Virgin Islands, 2nd Ed.
Vanuatu

Available from your favorite dive shop, bookstore, or directly from the publisher:
Pisces Books®, a division of Gulf Publishing Company, Book Division, Dept. AD, P.O.
Box 2608, Houston, Texas 77252-2608. (713) 520-4444.

Include purchase price plus $4.95 for shipping and handling. IL, NJ, PA, and TX residents add appropriate tax.